Lila

Lila

◆

A Biography

Kitty Katzell

iUniverse, Inc.
New York Lincoln Shanghai

Lila
A Biography

Copyright © 2006 by Mildred E. Katzell

iUniverse books may be ordered through booksellers or by contacting:

iUniverse
2021 Pine Lake Road, Suite 100
Lincoln, NE 68512
www.iuniverse.com
1-800-Authors (1-800-288-4677)

ISBN-13: 978-0-595-38973-5 (pbk)
ISBN-13: 978-0-595-83355-9 (ebk)
ISBN-10: 0-595-38973-2 (pbk)
ISBN-10: 0-595-83355-1 (ebk)

Printed in the United States of America

Contents

List of Illustrations

Cast of Characters

Lila, the heroine

Alta, Lila's younger sister

Anna, Lila's youngest sister

Elsie, Lila's older sister

Mabel, Lila's oldest sister

William Kehm, Lila's father

Anna Kehm, Lila's mother

Jenny Simpson Kehm, Lila's stepmother

Royce Engberg, Lila's first husband

Raymond Piper, Lila's second husband

Mildred Elaine, Lila and Royce's daughter

Jim Leonard, Mildred's first husband

Ray Katzell, Mildred's second husband

Cecil Harris, Alta's husband

Fanny Lenore, Alta and Cecil's daughter

Alfred Henry, Alta and Cecil's son

Fred Rolfe, Elsie's first husband

Henry Wolf, Elsie's second husband

FOREWORD

"Lila" is the biography of my mother, née Lila Gladys Kehm. When I was a child, I would ask her to tell me stories about her stepmother, much as other children ask a parent for a bedtime story. Later, when she was taking graduate courses, some of her professors required their students to write about their life experiences, and she kept these reports. Some of her relatives also asked her to write about certain episodes of which they had heard. Lila's younger sister, Alta, was interviewed on tape by Lenore, her daughter, about their home, family, and childhood. Then there was a box of clippings and notes that Lila had saved and from them I have gleaned additional information. All of these resources, and more, have served as the basis of the story reported here. Some are quoted verbatim from the records; others are paraphrased. Relatively little has been created from my own memories, except for the time of Lila's final years.

Kitty Katzell

Lila's Family, 1898—Mother, Mabel, Elsie, Father holding Lila

HOME AND FAMILY

Lila Gladys Kehm was born in Portland, Iowa, near Mason City on October 9, 1896. At that time, Portland was a cross-road village with a blacksmith shop, a one-room school, a small store, and a creamery, operated by her father. They lived very close to the school, so he took care of that, too. When she was three years old, he used to take her to the school and, while he was cleaning, she would "write" on the blackboard or on the floor with chalk. She was, apparently, his favorite and often received extra privileges.

Lila was the fourth of seven children, all born in Iowa, as were both of their parents. The first child was Mabel, who died when she was 12 years old. After Mabel, there was a boy, William, who died at the age of two weeks. Third was Elsie Louisa, who lived until 1985. Lila was fourth, followed by an unnamed "blue baby" who died after only ten days. The sixth child was Alta Pearl, who lived until 1989. Last was Anna, who died of pneumonia in 1920 at the age of 18. Anna's "first name" was Bernice but she was called "Anna" because that had been her mother's name. Many relatives had hoped that the new baby would be named for them, so her full given name was Bernice Anna Elizabeth Mary Ella Carrie Anne Kehm.

All four of their grandparents had been brought to the United States from Germany (Schlesswig-Holstein) when they were children. Lila's father was the eldest in a family of four boys and three girls. His father had died when he was a boy, leaving him to head the family and tend the Iowa farm. Lila's mother also lost her mother when she was a child, and she kept house for her father until she married.

Having come from Germany, Lila's parents, aunts, and uncles spoke German fluently. So Lila and the other children all learned German and they spoke only German until they went to school, because their father's mother lived with them and she spoke only German. Even after they went to school, the grace they said at meals was in German, as were their bedtime prayers. When her father spoke to other men and in many of his business dealings, he would speak in German. Relatives who visited also spoke German.

Lila's family moved from Iowa to Plankinton, South Dakota in 1901, when it was a "city" of some 800 residents. Her father wanted to get out of the creamery business and South Dakota was just opening up, so they went there. In Plankinton, he opened and operated a slaughter house and meat market, which meant they regularly had meat on the table. After the move to Plankinton, the girls were sometimes sent to visit relatives still in Mason City, Iowa, including their paternal grandmother and paternal aunts and uncles. They enjoyed these visits where they were warmly received with much affection and attention. Again, the language used in these visits was typically German.

The land around Plankinton was so flat that one could see for miles in all directions. There were no electric lights yet in Plankinton, but in Mitchell, which was 24 miles away, they had electricity. A big event of each evening was to go down to the railroad track and watch the lights come on in Mitchell. The railroad ran in a perfectly straight line and it was a thrill to see those lights from what seemed then to be a long distance away.

Every year in late summer after the crops had been harvested, day or night, there was the danger of prairie fires. Usually they were started by sparks flying from the train engines into the grasses along the tracks, but sometimes they were started by the careless dropping of matches or cigars. When there was a fire, everyone in town put on their oldest clothes and went out to fight it. Many times, the girls were sent home from school because the wind was strong and a prairie fire was not far away. Everyone used brooms with rags wrapped around them to beat out the flames and poured containers of water on the flames to douse them. If the weather was just right, the grass long enough, and the wind strong enough, the fire would creep closer and closer as people watched in horror. The men would try to plough as wide a swathe as possible between the fire and where people lived. The smoke and fumes made it difficult to breathe and everyone was very much afraid of the fires.

The same year that they moved to South Dakota, 1901, Lila's mother died on Friday, the 13th of June, following a hysterectomy and removal of an ovarian tumor. She developed peritonitis. Her death on Friday the 13th led to Lila's being superstitious about that date. The family had returned to Iowa for her mother to receive medical care, and there she died. Lila's aunt, her mother's maiden sister, returned with the family to South Dakota to keep house temporarily, but she was engaged to be married later that winter, so a housekeeper had to be found.

Lila's father advertised for a "hired girl" to come and take care of his home and five children. Only one person responded to his advertisement. In November, he went away and came back with their stepmother, Jenny Pitman Simpson. The children had not been told he was getting married. They were sitting at home waiting supper for him because the train was late, when he came in bringing a strange woman with him. He told the children they must call her "Mother". She came from Indiana, had been a nurse, had been married before, and had lived in Kentucky, where she had servants to wait on her. She had beautiful hands and wore many large rings—rings that inevitably struck the children when she slapped them, which was often. She spent much of her time reading love stories and giving orders to the children.

At this point it must be noted that Mabel, the eldest, was an epileptic who had seizures when she was excited or tense. She would become rigid and stop in her tracks till someone gave her a drink of water. After taking a drink, she would usually be all right and continue what she had been doing. Her stepmother was convinced that Mabel's seizures were nothing but temper and she was determined to "beat her out of them". As a result, she beat Mabel whenever she had a seizure. She also insisted that Mabel do chores just as the others did. On one occasion, she made Mabel carry a steaming kettle from the kitchen to the table. Mabel had a seizure which caused her to spill the scalding liquid on herself resulting in serious burns. Exactly one month to the day after their stepmother came into the house, Mabel died. She had not felt well when she wakened and wanted to stay in bed, but her stepmother insisted that she get up and do her share of the work. After lunch, Mabel lay down on the couch in the parlor. Then, later in the afternoon, she fell during a seizure. Water did not revive her that time, so Lila was sent for the doctor, who came, but Mabel could not be revived.

The house in Plankinton had been built after the family arrived in South Dakota. Alta and Lila remembered gathering pieces of wood shavings dropped by the men who were working on the house. They would stick the curly shavings in their hair and pretend they had curly golden locks. Years later, Elsie visited Plankinton and went to see the old house. The owner showed her around and finally asked her why there had been no closets in the original structure. Elsie explained that there had been a cupboard in the bedroom, and each girl had her own hook in the cupboard on which she hung the clothes she was not wearing. Later owners saw fit to add closets.

The house had no piped-in water. They were entirely dependent on the rain water that fell on the roof, which was piped down from the roof. Their Dad had built a box, attached to the house, and the water was piped to that. The box was a filter, filled with layers of stones and pebbles of graduated size. From the filter, the water ran into a cistern, which was a deep cemented hole in a lean-to behind the house. There was a pump with little cups mounted on a wheel that revolved drawing the water up. Every year, the cistern had to be emptied and cleaned before the rainy season started. By then, there wasn't much water left so what was left was scooped up, drawn to the top, and discarded. The cistern cleaning was a job with which the whole family had to help.

Elsie recalled that in the winter, when it was always bitter cold in South Dakota, they would pour kerosene down the drains to keep them from freezing.

The family grew their own vegetables, lettuce, radishes, beets, peas, and potatoes. Across from their house was an empty lot where someone had also planted potatoes, but its owner never came around to weed it or care for it. One Sunday, when the family was coming home from church, they were horrified to see a pathway of big potato bugs crossing the road from that potato bed to their own garden. The usual red potato bugs in that area could be killed by spraying them with "Paris Green", but these were Colorado beetles, which were bigger and yellow and black, and they weren't killed by "Paris Green." The children changed out of their "church clothes". Then each child was given a bucket and a stick with which to hit the potato plants and knock the beetles into the bucket, going up one row and down another. When they had half a bucket of beetles, they took them to the end of the garden where they dumped them into a pail of kerosene. When they were finished, their father struck a match to the kerosene.

Alta especially recalled the weeds in their vegetable patch, because it was her job to pull them up. She also recalled the peas. She loved peas, but Lila hated them, claiming they made her sick, but her stepmother insisted that she eat them. So Lila would put them in her mouth one at a time, like pills, and swallow them with a drink of water.

Breakfast was usually either cornmeal mush or oatmeal. Each was prepared by boiling the cereal in water with some salt, to which they then added milk and sugar—just a tiny bit of sugar, but as much milk as they wanted, because they kept their own cows. The children weren't allowed to have coffee or tea, but sometimes they were allowed to have hot water with a little milk and sugar added, and that was a special treat.

Every autumn, vendors would come to town. Then everyone would go down and buy up bags of apples and other produce and store them for the winter. When the weather was inclement and the children couldn't come home from school for lunch, each would take two slices of bread with golden syrup between, and, if there was an apple in the house, they'd also take an apple. The lunches were packed in the little tin buckets that the syrup had come in, and they carried those to school.

The evening meal often consisted of leftovers, and bread and butter, nothing very exciting. Sometimes there was hamburger mixed in with left over fried potatoes, and that was good. Meals were not fancy, but the girls thought that was because their stepmother didn't want to cook.

At every meal, three times a day, their stepmother sat at the head of the table with a willow stick at her place. To her right sat Anna, the baby, then their father and Lila. To their stepmother's left was Alta, then Elsie. The other end of the table was pushed up against the wall. Free use was made of the stick to impress upon the girls the proper use of their knives and forks. There was no table conversation other than "Pass this or that," "Lila, get some bread," "Elsie, don't put so much in your mouth," or "Take a bite of bread after every bite of meat or potato."

They learned never to smile for fear of getting the switch. As a result, Lila learned to bite the corners of her mouth to keep from smiling. In time, she developed a characteristic smile in which the corners of her mouth turned down, a feature that made her recognizable in her later years when her appearance had changed markedly.

The four girls all slept in one room, in two beds. Lila had charge of the alarm clock. When it went off, she was to jump out of bed, run to the dresser, and shut it off quickly before it wakened anyone else. One time, she awoke to find herself striking a match to light the lamp. She had jumped out of bed, run to the dresser and turned off the alarm without waking. The clock was always put on the dresser so she would have to get out of bed to shut off the alarm. She would then dress and waken the others.

They all dressed silently, making not a sound, and speaking only in whispers. When they were dressed, they crept downstairs. There were two steps that creaked, so they had to avoid stepping on them lest they wake their parents. For disturbing their stepmother's sleep, the girls would all get a beating as soon as the adults came downstairs.

Once downstairs, they would shut all the doors and creep around quietly. Each had her own chores for which she was responsible. They had to get the vegetables up from the cellar and peal them to be ready for dinner; empty the ashes from the night before; get in the wood and coal; start the fire; lay the breakfast table; and get the breakfast ready. Lila's chore was starting the fire in the big iron stove The fire was hard to start. The wood was often damp, or too big. Often she used the forbidden kerosene to start the fire, which blew the lids off the stove and burned her eyebrows and hair, but somehow she always got a fire started. She sometimes wondered if her father liked scorched cereal, as it seemed always to be scorched, sticky, or underdone, but he never complained.

Breakfast finished, Alta had to see that the beds were made and everything was tidy. After every meal, Lila and Elsie had to do the dishes. They had to pick them up without touching two together. Their stepmother was very nervous and given to headaches. She sat or stood over the girls as they stacked the dishes, just so; scraped them, just so; then washed them, just so. There was always a specified time limit for finishing each task. She warned them of the passing of the minutes and they were punished if the jobs were not done within the time limit. There were always plenty of chores to be done, and they were given explicit directions as to exactly how each was to be done, then watched to be sure they did it her way. When the cooking and cleaning were finished, there was always mending to be done.

When the morning chores were finished, the girls went off to the school, which was about a mile away. At noon, they had an hour to go home, eat lunch, do the dishes, and get back to school before the school bell stopped ringing. That meant they often had to run all the way back and there was often a freight train on the track across the sidewalk they took to school. One day, Lila crawled under a freight car and barely got through on the other side when the train started moving. Some local men saw what happened and told her dad how she was almost run over by the train, but he didn't scold her for doing it. The janitor at the school was kind and, if he saw the girls running to get back in time, he kept ringing the bell until he was sure they were in their seats.

After school, the girls helped their dad in the meat market. Lila and Elsie worked in the slaughter house; Alta delivered meat to the people who had placed orders. Her dad would put her on the wagon with the baskets of meat to be delivered, with labels to identify where they were to go.

Alta was able to ride horses before she could walk. There was a community cow pasture where residents could put their cows. They would take the cows there in the morning so they could eat all the grass they wanted, and then collect them at night and take them home. When she was still small, Alta was put on the horse and told to go and bring in the cows. Fortunately, the horse was experienced and could nose out the cow, so they usually got home safe and sound.

In the evening, after supper, the girls had homework to do. They all sat at the table with the oil lamp. Not only did they have no electricity, they also had no indoor plumbing. There were privies at the bottom of the garden, and a cistern outside in what they called the "shanty" where they pumped the water and where the tubs were kept for doing the wash

Once a week, they all got a bath. There was a round tub in which the clothes were washed on Mondays, but on Saturday bath night, it was brought into the kitchen. The reservoir on the side of the stove was filled with water and the fire was built up under it. There were also kettles of water heating on the stove. When all of the water was hot, it was poured into the tub and the girls took turns getting in, getting scrubbed, and getting out, so the next one could get into the same tub, have her bath and get out. Then they all put on their nightgowns and went off to bed.

Lila's Family, 1906—Anna, Father, Elsie, Alta, Lila, Stepmother

CHILDHOOD INCIDENTS

When the family was still living in Portland, Lila's particular friend was a neighbor boy at whose home she used to play in the afternoon. They used to play house, and she would wash and iron. He had a toy flat iron that he gave her when the family moved to South Dakota.

◆   ◆   ◆

Lila was probably about five years old when she and Elsie strayed on their way home from school in Portland. Their mother was entertaining the Ladies Aid Society that afternoon and was serving ice cream and cake. It was a lovely day, so instead of going directly home from school, the girls walked to the railroad tracks to pick flowers. They had their arms full of lovely blossoms when they looked up and saw their father coming toward them with a stick in his hand. He didn't beat them but took each of them by an ear and led them home without a word. There he put them in the cellar to wait until the guests were gone. They sat on the cellar steps and pinched each other and stepped on each other's toes. When the guests were gone, they were put to bed without supper, and without ice cream and cake.

◆   ◆   ◆

In school, they had a teacher whose name was Cad Florence. Miss Florence would not allow the children to speak the German they spoke at home, so once they got to school, they had to speak English. Miss Florence also tried very hard to break Elsie of being left-handed. Finally, her father told Miss Florence, "We have tried to break her of that habit for six years and it hasn't worked. Now, you try to teach her something, and leave her left hand alone.

◆   ◆   ◆

The Kehm household was always absolutely temperate. There was never anything alcoholic in the house, not even a bottle of brandy for medicinal use. On rare occasions, Vanilla Essence was used to relieve pain because it was the one form of alcohol that was allowed in the house.

◆   ◆   ◆

In South Dakota, the family preserved a lot of fruit and vegetables every year. Anything they had in the garden was preserved and put down in the cellar. There was also a bin in one corner of the cellar where they stacked great piles of potatoes. When spring came, the potatoes would begin to sprout. If the sprouts were not removed, all the goodness of the potatoes went into the sprouts and there would be no potatoes to eat nor even any for planting. So, when the potatoes began to sprout, the girls were sent down to the cellar where they had to take out each potato, one at a time, and tear off all the sprouts before adding that potato to the pile of those whose sprouts had been removed.

One time, Lila and Alta were down in the cellar doing the job of removing the potato sprouts. It was a very hot job and they were very tired and thirsty. Lila took a look around to see if she could find something they could drink. Somewhere up in the eaves, over in a corner, she found a bottle of grape juice they had once preserved. She got the bottle open and they shared it. It tasted a bit strange, but they thought it was quite good, so they finished the bottle and hid it away so nobody would know they had found it.

Eventually someone shouted for them to come up for supper and added, "Bring up that pan of milk when you come; we need it for supper." So Lila made Alta go up first, carrying the pan of milk. Just as she got to the top of the stairs and started across the floor, Alta fell down flat and the milk went all over the floor. The family all thought she had been working too hard as she felt somewhat feverish. They never suspected, and Alta and Lila never told, about the bottle of grape juice.

◆   ◆   ◆

The most important entertainment of the year took place when the circus came to town. They came on a special train that was filled with the animals, the tents, and the people. Then everything was shifted off the train into trucks. First thing in the morning, the girls would look out their window to see the site where the tent was set up. They had great fun watching how they got down the tents, and the men came along and pounded in the stakes, and then the carriages came up full of the animals, and it was all very exciting. After that, they could look forward to the time when they could go and see the circus. That was about the only time they ever did anything "special."

◆   ◆   ◆

Their father was a very strict Methodist who thought theater-going was very bad indeed. The girls remembered one evangelist who preached about a theater that had had a fire while a play was being performed. People were trapped in the theater and burned to death. The preacher said that they had gone straight to Hell because they never should have been there.

◆   ◆   ◆

When Lila was in high school, she entered an elocution contest. One of the topics on which she spoke was the spider web of the Brooklyn Bridge. She won a silver medal for her talk. Elsie remembered her standing on the stage of the local opera house, as it was called, and giving her talk.

◆   ◆   ◆

Lila's mother believed that Lila had a special guardian angel taking care of her. One time when she was still a baby, Lila crawled out onto the road and was playing in the mud when a run-away horse and buggy came down the road. Mabel, her eldest sister, snatched Lila out of the road in the nick of time. There was also the time that she had crawled under the freight car to get to school on time, and the train started moving, but she got through safely.

◆   ◆   ◆

Whenever their stepmother would go away, even to a neighbor's or out for an afternoon, as soon as she was gone the girls felt free to relax and have fun. But one of them always stood guard for her return so they could be busy when she arrived. If they knew she would be gone for several hours, or for a day, they undertook real projects. They might make a batch of candy and eat the whole thing. Or they would play with something they had been forbidden to touch, like the sewing machine.

One time it was the bacon slicer. Alta was trying to get the last slices from a slab of bacon and Lila thought she was making a big fuss about it. Lila grabbed the handle to take over, but Alta's finger was too near the blade and a piece of her left middle finger was sliced off and left dangling by a bit of skin. The two girls pushed the piece back on and bound it up with a bandage, and eventually it grew back on. It left a deep scar which remained puffed up, but Alta always claimed it was useful because when she was told to raise her left hand, she knew that was the hand with the scar on it. Of course, they made sure their stepmother never heard about the incident.

◆   ◆   ◆

Another time while their stepmother was away, Anna poked beans up her nose and couldn't get them out. The older girls tried everything, until finally Lila had the bright idea of sprinkling pepper on the stove. That made Anna sneeze and the beans popped out.

◆   ◆   ◆

Anna—Age 6 years, 9 months

Anna had lovely long hair, as can be seen in the accompanying picture. Her three older sisters, Elsie, Lila, and Alta, would compete to see who would get to brush it. That was a special treat for them and they would gladly spend hours doing it.

◆   ◆   ◆

The girls loved anything that took them away from their home and step-mother, whether it was school, working for a neighbor, helping their dad at the meat market, or anything else. Those things were a blessing, a release from tor-ture.

Lila was her father's regular helper at the meat market. Almost every day they had to kill a cow and often a pig, too. When school was out, she would rush home and change clothes to go to the slaughter house. She could skin a cow in 45 minutes and, if she didn't cut a hole in the hide, he paid her 25¢, which she put into savings toward college. If she didn't help her father on Saturday, she worked helping more affluent families. For a day's work from 8 a.m. to 7 p.m. she was paid 75¢. In a normal day, she would do the week's wash by hand with a scrub-bing board, hang it out to dry, iron it with a flat iron heated on the stove, and clean the house. But to her it was freedom, and she learned a lot from the women for whom she worked. Eventually, she got as much as $1 for a 10-hour day.

She tried to save all of her money for college, but her stepmother often took it as fines for some misdemeanor or as a loan, which she promptly forgot and never repaid.

◆   ◆   ◆

One time a photographer came to Plankinton, taking stamp-size pictures of people very inexpensively. So everyone was having pictures taken. When their father told Alta to go and get her picture taken, she refused. He asked why, and she told him she didn't want a picture with a huge sore on her face. When he asked how she got the sore, she told him, "That's where your wife hits me with her big fat ring."

Lila had a similar experience. Sometimes her father took her when he drove out into the country to buy cows or pigs. When she was in high school, one time she had an ugly scar on her cheek. Her father commented that she had always had such a nice complexion and he wondered how she got the scar. She broke down and told him how her stepmother hit her and the other girls with her hand with the heavy wide rings. He said, "Lila, you're as strong as she is; don't let her do it." She was shocked, but from then on things started to change. The very next day, when her stepmother lifted her hand to strike her as she cleared the table, Lila's pulse quickened, her knees shook, but she calmly held her stepmother's hand and prevented the blow.

In addition to the welts on their cheeks, the girls usually had scabs or sores on their ears from their stepmother's twisting them. They also had welts on their backs and legs from the strap she used to beat them.

◆   ◆   ◆

Their stepmother would buy material to make one of the girls a new dress. Then, with fiendish glee, she would give it to one of her nieces because the girls had been what she called "ornery".

◆   ◆   ◆

Sometimes their stepmother would forget to punish the girls for something that had happened during the day. Then, when they were in bed and asleep, she would go up and get them out of bed to give them a strapping. That usually happened when there had been company, and she was always on good behavior when there was company.

◆   ◆   ◆

The girls often went to school in clothes of which they were ashamed. When Lila was in her early teens, one Sunday in Sunday School a lady asked if Lila could help her with some housework since she was not well. Lila was happy to do it. The lady made two dresses for Lila the year she was a freshman in high school and, for the first time, she was not ashamed of her appearance when she went to school.

◆   ◆   ◆

One of Lila's neighbors had a baby boy and Lila used to sneak over to take care of him. She would work hard just to have a chance to stay there. She would iron for the neighbor and talk to the baby. Her cup of joy overflowed when the baby's first word was not "Mama" but "Lila."

◆   ◆   ◆

One year, Lila's only gift in her Christmas stocking was a bundle of sticks. Not surprisingly, she cried. When she was offered a book to console her, she refused it. She refused also to eat any of the Christmas candy and nuts because she was so hurt.

◆   ◆   ◆

Twice when things were unusually dark, Lila contemplated suicide. She even hid a bottle of carbolic acid in the garden. She would have drunk it but she had compassion on her sisters, for she knew their stepmother would be just that much meaner to them.

◆   ◆   ◆

Lila had received no sex education at home, and certainly none at school. She knew nothing about menstruation, so when she began to menstruate, she was scared. She didn't know what to do, so she burned her soiled clothing so no one would know about it. Before long, she told Elsie what had happened. Since Elsie was older she had found out what was going on so she was able to tell Lila.

◆   ◆   ◆

When Lila was about ten years old, she was often sent into town for the evening mail. To go to town from their house, she had to cross the railroad tracks, pass a pool hall, a livery stable, two saloons, and a vacant lot. The evening train came in late enough so that it was usually dark when she got home and there were no street lights along most of the way so she had a dreadful fear of someone grabbing her or chasing her.

One night, she was about to step off the sidewalk to cut across the vacant lot on her way home when a man suddenly stepped in front of her and punched her low in the abdomen. She screamed and ran for home.

Another night when she was returning from school, she heard a tapping on a window as if to attract someone's attention. When she looked up, she saw a naked man standing in front of the hotel window masturbating.

On one occasion, when her folks were out for the evening and the girls were all sitting around the dining table studying, Lila looked toward the window and saw a man peering in at them.

◆   ◆   ◆

At some point when Lila was a teenager, her father bought a car. The salesman showed him how to drive it and also gave him a book of instructions. When he got the car home, he told Lila he was going to take a nap and when he got up, he'd show her how to drive it. So, while he took his nap, she read the book of instructions and proceeded to take the car out for a ride. When she got back, she parked the car under his bedroom window and honked the horn. Her dad looked out the window and said, "You think you're pretty smart, don't you?"

◆   ◆   ◆

When Lila was a senior in high school, her stepmother took a trip home to Indiana to visit her mother and, shortly after her return, a man came to the house to visit her. She said he was an old friend of her first husband. Lila was as ignorant as a 16-year-old could be, but when she came home from church and saw him coming out of her stepmother's bedroom, she knew something was going on.

The man pretended to take a fancy to Lila. He praised her cooking and asked her to come out to Oregon and live with his daughter. He would even send her to college. But she disliked him. He tried to kiss her when he left, but Lila repulsed him and was scolded for it later by her stepmother.

After he left, her stepmother received letters from him. By this time, Lila had learned to sneak. She read the letters and found that they set forth a plan for their stepmother to leave Lila's dad, but first she would get a settlement from him. Lila told her dad and they laid a trap. They discovered that the man was in the white slave traffic and not a friend of the stepmother's first husband at all. It even sounded from the letters like they were planning to sell the girls into slavery.

EARLY WORK EXPERIENCE

Throughout her early life, Lila planned on going to college and being a teacher. When she played games, she was always 'teacher'. Who would ever have thought that a girl out on the South Dakota prairies would dream of going to college to be a teacher, when few boys or girls even finished high school in those days? Her father said if she wanted to go to college, he'd help as he could but she would have to support herself. She had saved every penny she could, so when the time came, she had a total of $200. She had also studied hard and was Valedictorian when she graduated from high school, so she got a 4-year scholarship to attend Dakota Wesleyan University in Mitchell, South Dakota. In those days, tuition was under $100 a semester.

She had dreamed of college and, from reading books, she thought she would have a wonderful social life while getting an education. However, she was not what was called a "favored applicant" for a job in the college—doing dishes, working in the library, and that sort of thing—so she had to live off the campus and work in someone's home for her room and board. As a result, she had no social life, and no money for "Societies" (there were no fraternities or sororities).

Each year at the University, there was a week known as Religious Emphasis with a special speaker who led the daily Chapel Services and special evening meetings. Daily chapel attendance was compulsory at the University. One evening, the speaker said that God has a plan for each person, and cited Matthew 6:6 ff as the Bible reference for that statement. To discover His plan, the minister said, "Go into your room and close the door. Pray, asking God to reveal His plan for your life, promising to 'do whatever, to go wherever and whenever' He calls. Pray on your knees till you receive His answer."

That night, Lila went to her room in the home where she was working for her room and board and did just as the speaker had suggested. She turned off the light, got down on her knees in her cold room, and prayed for guidance. She prayed hard and long, and she felt that God had answered her. He said very clearly that He wanted her to be a missionary. This occurred in 1915-16, when she was a sophomore. She then joined the Student Volunteer Movement, and wrote to tell her father about her experience.

During the summer following her junior year, Lila worked at a college camp. It was a broadening experience for her, and for once, she really enjoyed herself. She graduated after four years, in 1918, some $200 in debt, having had a rugged experience with very little fun.

The day after she came home from college, a neighbor, who was president of the local bank and probably the richest man in town, came over to her house and told her he wanted her to come and work in the bank as assistant bookkeeper and cashier. She told him she had prepared to teach, not to do commercial work. He said, "I know. We'll teach you. You'll begin on Monday." And she did. It was another opportunity to learn! Besides, her father and little sister, Anna, needed her help at home so she couldn't leave Plankinton.

Lila had always had the idea that bankers' hours were short, but she worked six days a week. This was early in 1918. There were Liberty Bonds to sell, federal income tax for the first time, and an unprecedented land boom. There were no wonderful electric or electronic machines to do the computations. The only machines they had were an adding machine and a manual posting machine that had just been acquired. Banking hours were 9 A.M. to 4 P.M., but Lila opened the bank and started work at 8 A.M. (and often earlier) and went home when the books were balanced, sometimes 6 P.M. or later. She learned a lot and worked long and hard, six days a week, even going in on holidays—Washington's Birthday, July Fourth, etc.—because she had to figure the interest on savings accounts and there was always something that needed to be done. She took not a single day's vacation and had no holidays. They didn't tell her to come in on holidays, but she knew it was her work and she was responsible.

Her starting pay was $75 per month. The banker had said when he hired her that he would increase her pay when she had learned the job and was worth more. After more than a year with no increase in pay, Lila was approached to teach History, English, and Algebra in the local high school. Her pay would be $110 per month for nine months. She told the bank president and the cashier that she was taking the job, and reminded them that they had promised to pay her more when she had learned the job and was worth it. During her last month at the bank, she was paid an additional $25, but she didn't change her mind about leaving. One of her former high school classmates took the job in the bank.

Lila taught at the high school in Plankinton for two years, from 1919 to 1921. In 1920, Anna, her youngest sister, died in the flu epidemic. It was a particular shock for Lila because Anna was not only her baby sister, she was also a pupil in several of Lila's classes. Lila had always been a mother to her.

Many of Anna's friends were also in Lila's classes, which was not easy for them nor for Lila. She discussed the complexity of the situation frankly with the students and, though they were on a first-name basis outside of school, they never tried to take advantage in school. In fact, they seemed to share the responsibility of trying to help her to make good.

During the summer months when Lila was teaching in Plankinton, she used to tutor students who had failed a subject or were making up a missing credit in order to graduate.

In 1920, Lila's father also died rather suddenly. By this time, he had sold the butcher shop and become a real estate agent. There was a lot of farm land in Plankinton at that time, and quite a lot of business came that way, so he earned enough to keep the family going. He and his wife had separated, but she had occasionally returned to Plankinton. She had been promiscuous and had contracted gonorrhea, for which the family doctor had been treating her for some time, but the doctor had never warned her husband. As a result on one of her visits home, he contracted the disease and died as a consequence of her promiscuity. While gonorrhea is not regarded as a fatal illness, the girls felt that he died of the shame of the disease.

The girls had thought they were quite well off when their father died. The family had many sections of land, but it was mortgaged, and there was plenty of insurance. However, in a few years, the insurance was gone from paying interest and taxes, and there were no crops, so they lost the land. The house had been left to their stepmother, so the girls had to find other places to live.

Lila moved to a friend's home for her last year in Plankinton. It was at about this time that she applied to the Woman's Foreign Missionary Society (WFMS) of the Methodist Church to be sent out as a missionary. She was tentatively accepted and as soon as things were cleared up at home, she expected that she would be sent to Java. She had some doubts about going to Java because she had had a minor heat stroke at one time and Java would be hot, but so was South Dakota.

In 1921, Lila left Plankinton and went to Webster, South Dakota to teach English. It was while she was living there that she met Royce Raymond Engberg, to whom she would be married in 1922.

Lila, Alta, & Elsie, 1963

ELSIE LOUISA KEHM

Lila's older sister, Elsie, didn't want to go to college so she moved out of Plankinton when she finished high school and taught school. She lived with a Norwegian couple, Mr. & Mrs. Fred Rolfe, in a house that was quite near to the school because school teachers were expected to start the fire in the schoolhouse in the morning, clean the school, and get everything ready, in addition to the teaching. Elsie stayed in that job for three years and then decided to take up nurses' training. She went to Mitchell and studied at the Methodist State Hospital until she came down with the flu and had to discontinue her studies.

One story she told about her nursing education may describe an experience that is familiar to others who have studied to become nurses. The class was being taught how to give a patient a bed bath. They were told to use a wash cloth to wash the patient's arms, back, and abdomen. Then, still using the washcloth, they were told they should wash the patient's legs up as far as possible. The instructor paused at that point before adding, "Then give him the wash cloth and let him wash possible."

While Elsie was in nurses' training, Mrs. Rolfe died, and Fred Rolfe moved to Mitchell. At that time, Mitchell was not a very big place, so Elsie and Fred met quite frequently and within a short time, on March 9, 1918, they were married. After their marriage, they both worked for a relative of Fred's who was a florist. One Saturday in 1928, Fred came into the florist shop and said he couldn't stay, he felt so ill. Saturday night was the shop's busiest night, so Elsie couldn't get away. When she finally got home, she found Fred was very ill. Eventually she was able to get the doctor to come to the house and he didn't know what was wrong with Fred. After only a day or two, Fred died. They did a post mortem and, as Alta reported, they were told the cord in the back of his neck had snapped, which Alta thought very unlikely.

Elsie sold their house in Mitchell, moved into an apartment in town, and got another girl to share the apartment. The other girl was a hairdresser. Elsie continued to work in the florist shop. They got along well, had a lot in common, and went places together.

On a vacation in 1929, Elsie went to Alaska with a friend (perhaps the room-mate). As an 8-year-old child, she had heard a missionary talk about Alaska and had wanted to go there ever since. She had once been on a Pullman, but she had never been in a dining car. She didn't know how to order a meal. She recalled that her first meal on the train was a pineapple and cottage cheese salad.

First she toured Yellowstone Park, then went on to Seattle where she took a room at the Atwood Hotel because she had heard that Alaskans stayed there. From Seattle, she went north on the Yukon steamer bound for Whittier. On the first day out, she and her friend were walking on the deck when another passenger approached and asked if they played cards. Elsie's friend said, "No, but Elsie does."

Elsie said, "Oh, just a very little."

The man said, "Well, you come with me."

The man was Henry Wolf and he had a stateroom on the top deck They played cards ("500") all the way to Alaska. It turned out he was returning to Alaska from a trip to Yellowstone, and they had been there at the same time. They parted company at Cordova, and Elsie went on to Kennecot where she stayed for a week, before going on to Fairbanks. Her friend stayed in Kennecot with her husband who was working there. From Fairbanks Elsie went by train through McKinley (now Denali) Park on the way to Anchorage. In Anchorage, she stayed at the Anchorage Hotel for two weeks. She really had gone to Anchorage to look for work. She applied at Jones Grocery store, but was told she wasn't strong enough to work there, so she waited in Anchorage for the next boat going south.

During her stay in Anchorage, Henry Wolf took her out to dinner several times and they went on a 20-mile drive in Henry's Whippet almost every day. The 20-mile drive was all the roads they had in Anchorage at that time. Henry told Elsie that he had reached retirement age and he was looking to find someone to be his housekeeper or to marry. He intended to buy a house and he would need someone to keep house for him. He had cataracts and couldn't drive a car any more, so he would need someone to drive him about him as well as any of his friends who might visit. And he would want a place with at least one extra bedroom so that any of his friends coming out of Alaska would have a place to stay with him. His family were all farmers in Iowa. In 1898, he had had TB and was so ill they thought he wouldn't survive the winter, which was why he had gone to Alaska where he would benefit from the germ-free air.

Elsie also learned that Henry had come to Alaska in 1898 in the gold rush and was a member of the "Pioneers of Alaska.". He had made friends with a man named Henry Pope, who had an office in Dawson, and, in 1915, the two men went to a place called Ship Creek, because the government was going to build a railroad and establish a city at the head of Cook Inlet.

Mr. Pope decided that the most likely place for the city to be built was on the hill above the creek, so he left Henry to go to the auction of property lots while he went to Seattle to get supplies to start their business. So Henry went to the auction, and on the second day, bought the lot at 5th and C for $400 and they set up their business in a double tent with a plank floor. The name of the business was "Pioneer Sheet Metal Works." Each week, they each took $25 to live on, for clothing, meals, savings, everything. Mr. Pope did all the metal work and Henry handled all the financial aspects. Each of them thought the other was just right.

Henry sold his half of the business to Mr. Pope on January 1, 1930 for $15,000. It was still a double tent. In 1936, Mr. Pope sold out to Ray Wolf, one of Henry's nephews. In 1945, Ray and his brother Bob opened the new Wolfes Department Store in a very modern, two-story building on the same corner of 5th and C lot.

Now back to Elsie's trip to Alaska. She returned to the "lower 48"—Seattle, Portland, San Francisco, and Los Angeles. She stayed with friends in Los Angeles for a time before taking a train to New Orleans, from Long Beach, CA, and then to Stillwater, OK, to visit a cousin. A man she had worked for in a grocery store in Mitchell wanted her to come back to work, but she owned a house in Mitchell from which she received rental income, and she had some money in the bank that she could live on, so she delayed going back to work for five or six weeks.

At Christmas time that year, Elsie heard from Henry for the first time. With his letter, he enclosed a check for $100 and told her to buy something for herself for Christmas. She went out and bought herself a diamond ring. After that, they wrote back and forth all the time until he finally wrote and asked her to marry him. Neither of them had a telephone so he asked her in a letter. Henry was 30 years older than Elsie, but she had no qualms at all about marrying him. She packed up and got ready to go.

Elsie thought it was really exciting, going to Alaska to live. She was getting away from South Dakota. She packed her bag and arranged to have her furniture shipped by boat to Alaska.

It was 1930. Lila and Mildred had been in America on furlough and they were heading west to sail from Los Angeles, so Elsie drove them in her DeSoto to Los Angeles. From there, one of Elsie's friends drove the DeSoto to Seattle, and Elsie went by boat. Henry was waiting for her in Seattle and the second she was there, he told her he had sold his business in Alaska and they were going to live in Seattle. She was quite disappointed because she had wanted to go to the "last frontier". She didn't know anyone in Seattle. Henry had a brother there and knew a few other people, but she didn't know a soul.

They had planned to be married on January 15, which was Henry's birthday. But Elsie arrived at 5 p.m. on that date so everything was already closed. For some reason, Elsie said she wouldn't be married on Friday or Saturday, so they were finally married on January 20, 1930. A teller at the bank and the taxi driver stood up with them. The taxi driver asked where they usually went to church and Elsie replied, "In South Dakota, I always went to the Presbyterian Church." So he took them there and then he stood up with them. As it turned out, the day they were married was the anniversary of Henry's parents' marriage.

After the wedding, the minister took Elsie aside and said, "Now see that he does the dishes the very first day." She said, "All right." So the next morning after breakfast, she left the dishes on the table and didn't say anything about it.

Finally Henry asked, "When are you going to do the dishes?"

Elsie replied, "When are WE going to do the dishes? You're supposed to dry them."

He said, "I never dried a dish in my life."

She said, "Then we'll just leave the dirty dishes right there." She wasn't going to wash the dishes if he wasn't going to help. Eventually, they did wash the dishes and Henry asked her never to tell his brothers. She promised never to tell anyone he ever did anything about the housework, so Henry wiped the dishes from then on.

Henry told Elsie they were not going on a wedding trip, because she had just had her trip to Seattle and he had had his boat trip from Alaska. So they went to Portland, Oregon, for a few days.

Back in Seattle, Henry said they should not be in a rush to buy a house, so they lived on the fifth floor of the Blanchard Hotel at 5th and Blanchard for a while. It was close to the banks and anything else they needed. One day, Elsie took the elevator down from their room and when she got off the elevator she was crying.

Henry said, "What in the world is wrong with you?"

She said, "There was a drunk man on the elevator."

Henry asked, "Did he say anything to you?"

Elsie said, "Yes, he asked me what my name was and where I lived, and I told him I lived right here."

So the next week, they started looking for a house. Henry said they couldn't live in a place where they kept drunk people. They looked for a house for about a week before they bought the house at 9020 Fifth Avenue, NE. At the time, the area was a mess because a man from Fairbanks had built 28 houses on the block of land, and it was still a mud pile. They moved into the house on February 22, 1930, Washington's birthday.

Lila and Elsie were never close, although, as long as they lived, the three sisters, Elsie, Lila and Alta, made it a practice to write to each other once a week, as their father had insisted they do when they first started to leave home. On one occasion, Elsie joined Lila and Mildred for some vacation at Clear Lake, Iowa, where they rented a cottage for a week. After two days, Elsie got in her car and left. She and Lila couldn't be under the same roof for extended periods. She did, eventually, return but she had a hot temper and she found it better to leave the situation than to try to repair the damage she would have done by remaining.

Lila had quite a reputation in her family for her baking. Elsie had tried unsuccessfully on numerous occasions to make one of the cakes that Lila often made. So one time, when Lila and Mildred were visiting Elsie and Henry at their home in Seattle, the two of them made the same cake at the same time. Again, Lila's cake turned out fine; Elsie's cake was a failure. The sisters finally decided it must be because of Elsie's extreme left-handedness. They could find no other explanation.

After their marriage, Henry went on many fishing trips up into Canada, mostly to Lake Hyum and Loon Lake. At Hyum, he and his friends fished for salmon; at Loon Lake, for trout. To get to Lake Hyum, they had to go the last nine miles on horseback. There, they stayed in an Indian camp in a little old cabin. They got their water from the lake and went out back to the bathroom. There was nothing modern there, and no white people, only Indians.

Needless to say, Elsie and Henry also made many return trips to Alaska.

When they were first married, Henry had told Elsie that she would always be provided for, but that the bulk of his estate would go to his family. That was acceptable to Elsie. As he grew old and needed a lot of care and attention, Elsie was always diligent and faithful and cared for him with utter devotion, so he changed his will and left everything to her.

Henry had been born on January 15, 1867. He died on October 7, 1966.

She had sold their house in 1962, when it became necessary for Henry to receive care in a nursing home. She spent her last days at The Hearthstone, a continuing care retirement community in Seattle.

Elsie was born February 28, 1895. She died on April 8, 1985.

ALTA PEARL KEHM

Lila and her younger sister, Alta, were very close throughout their lives. Some has already been written about their relationship in the first two chapters and more will appear in later chapters.

When Alta was nine years old, she contracted meningitis (probably meningo-coccal meningitis which sometimes occurs in epidemics and usually affects chil-dren). She related it to an incident in school. The school had seats that could be raised when the pupil stood up. One time when she stood up to answer a ques-tion, she stood to one side without raising the seat. The boy behind her put his foot around and raised the seat. As a result, she fell to the floor when she went to sit down, and she injured her back.

Her stepmother had been a nurse and continued to provide nursing care to people who were ill in order to earn pocket money. At the time of Alta's fall, she was nursing a boy who had meningitis. A few days after her fall, Alta lay down in the afternoon and fell asleep. She felt very tired. When they called her to come to eat, she recalled going into the room and seeing everyone sitting at the table, and then she fell. She probably fainted.

Later she was told that she had been very sick and had had "spinal meningi-tis." She didn't know how long she was sick but she was aware of being on a cot in the dining room. She thought she was running along a narrow road in a forest, trying to dodge the trees. She didn't know where she was going, but she felt that she had to get out of that place. Suddenly ahead of her, she saw a tiny light, so she tried to run to get there. Then she heard someone crying and she thought some-one must be in trouble so she should run even faster, always trying to avoid the trees and increase her speed. Finally the light grew wider and, when she opened her eyes, she found she was in the dining room, the light was on, and her father was kneeling beside her, crying. Later she learned that the doctor had said she couldn't possibly last the night. She must have turned the corner and soon she began to get better.

Alta attended Dakota Wesleyan University in Mitchell, South Dakota. She worked for her room and board in the home of a lawyer and his wife. The wife was a society lady and they often went out at night, so they wanted someone to live in to be a baby sitter. She also did the dishes after each meal, cleaned the rooms that they let out in their home, and did general cleaning and dusting. The wife was a good cook, the food was always good, and Alta enjoyed their company.

One morning, Alta woke up and thought she was going to die! The people where she lived contacted the college and were told to take Alta over there. They had cleared out a whole section of the college and filled it with beds. There were two nurses there taking care of everyone. When Alta was able to leave, she went home to Plankinton to recuperate. She had had the flu, during one of the major epidemics. Anna, her youngest sister, was still at home. She probably contracted the flu from Alta. She was the only one in the family who succumbed to it.

As she reported in a taped conversation with her daughter, Lenore Burt:

There were always a lot of missionaries returning from India and other parts of the world. They came and gave speeches to us and told us all about their countries. I sort of had an inkling in my brain that I'd like to leave America and do something entirely different. So I put my name down as soon as I finished college to get a job abroad.

I was finally chosen to go to India. I didn't choose India. I just wanted to travel, go abroad, continue teaching, become the head of a school.

She was eventually selected to become the "manageress" of a large girls' school in Lahore, which was then in India, now in Pakistan. Alta was there when she got word that Lila's husband, Royce, had died. Lila was distraught. She wrote the most pathetic letters to Alta telling how upset she was. She said she was suffering with boils that made her really ill. Alta felt very sorry for her and decided that what Lila needed was to get into a job, but she realized that was difficult with Mildred on her hands needing to be taken care of all the time and every day. Alta concluded that it might be best for Lila to come to India, if they could find a place where the climate would be safe for Mildred. It couldn't be a place near Alta, because the weather on the plains was severe all year round. She decided Darjeeling would be an ideal location, so she wrote to the treasurer of the mission and told the whole story about Lila and Royce, their plans to be missionaries, his death, and their baby daughter. She sent copies of the letter to the president of Dakota Wesleyan, who had known Lila as a student, and to others that she thought would be influential.

Alta didn't know what was happening until, some weeks later, she received a letter from Lila who was already in Port Said on her way to India. Lila and Mildred came directly to Lahore and they had a short visit before leaving for Darjeeling.

Near the middle of Alta's fourth year in Lahore, there was a death at another girls' boarding school in Ajmer and there was no one to fill the vacancy. Alta had already had another young woman sent to her to be trained to fill her position while she was on a forthcoming furlough. It was decided that her trainee had received enough training, making Alta available to go to Ajmer to fill the other position.

In Ajmer, there was a large settlement of English and American missionaries and engineers. Henry Cecil Harris was working on the railway, and he was white and English and there weren't many of them, so they all used to go to the club where they played tennis and entertained together. After a year, Alta and Cecil, as he was called, became engaged, and six months later, they were married. Alta was nearing the end of her contract term in India, so the mission released her a few months early and didn't deduct it from her pay, which was important. Mildred, Lila's daughter, was flower girl at the wedding.

On February 6, 1930, in Ajmer, India, Alta gave birth to a daughter, Fanny Lenore. Lila and Mildred were visiting when Lenore, as she was called, was born. They were on their way back to America on furlough.

When next Lila and Mildred saw Alta, it was 1935 in England. By then Alta had a son, Alfred who was born on June 15, 1933. The family lived on Oakwood Crescent in Sudbury Town, Greenford, Middlesex. On the day after they arrived at Alta's home, 5-year-old Lenore took 11-year-old Mildred to Sunday School with her. Mildred was to wait for Lenore in a specified location in the church so they could walk home together. When her class let out, Mildred went to that location and waited what seemed to her a long time, but Lenore didn't come, so she thought Lenore must have forgotten and she would have to find her way home somehow. Meantime, when Lenore arrived at the designated site and couldn't find Mildred, she went home and told Alta. In Lenore's words, Alta went berserk. Lenore couldn't understand why it was such a problem because it was such an easy journey between Sunday School and home and Mildred was such a big girl. They set out and soon found Mildred walking along the street weeping. Again, Lenore was shocked, because big girls didn't cry!

Mildred went to school during the three months that she and Lila stayed with Alta's family. Because her early education had been in the British system, the transition was not difficult. In one of her classes, the teacher had her tell the class where she had been, including the trips back and forth between America and India. When she finished, the teacher said, "Do you know what we call someone like you?" Mildred didn't know. The teacher said, "A globetrotter."

In 1939, Cecil embarked to India to take up the position of governor of the Calcutta Electricity Company. Alta and the children followed in due course, but got only as far as Madras before they received a message to disembark and wait there for Cecil, so they could return to England on the next ship. Concern for his health and the fact that the job had not been what he had expected had led to his decision. This was 1939 and the return trip through the Mediterranean was a stressful journey, during which the ship flew the ensign at all times. It was the time when Italy was taking over Albania. The ship made an unscheduled stop in Marseilles, France, and many passengers disembarked and completed their journey by train through France.

When they reached England, Alta and her family lived for several months in rented rooms in Kew Gardens, near where Cecil's mother was living. Soon after war was declared, they moved to Richmond, where they were living when the family was bombed out. For a few weeks they stayed with friends. In late 1940, Cecil's job was evacuated to Lancashire, and they were there for about nine months until he was moved again to Bath, where they remained until the war was over. During that time, Cecil was responsible for the air conditioning of a large quarry where many of the country's treasures were stored.

In 1945, the family moved back to London to a large Victorian house in Kew Gardens. There, Alta rented rooms to students studying at the nearby Royal Botanical Gardens. When Cecil retired in 1965, he and Alta moved to Eastbourne. By that time, both children were married and settled elsewhere. Cecil died in 1978 and Alta continued to live in their home in Eastbourne. She died on April 9, 1988.

Throughout her adult life, Alta's interests were centered around her church. She also very much enjoyed gardening and was an avid reader.

Royce, 1922

Lila, 1922

FIRST MARRIAGE

In the summer of 1921, Lila was living in Webster, South Dakota, and tutoring boys and girls who had failed a subject or who were making up a credit in order to graduate.

On the afternoon of July 21, she looked out the kitchen window and saw a young man coming to the house where she was rooming. She just knew he was going to be a salesman! Since she was making sandwiches to take on a picnic later that day, she went to the door with the bread-knife in her hand so he would realize she was busy. He was good looking, very polite, and most apologetic for bothering her. He asked if he could make an appointment to come and speak with her the next morning. She knew she would be tutoring at 10:00 a.m., so she suggested he come at 9:00, and then promptly forgot all about him.

The next morning when the doorbell rang at 9 a.m., her long hair was not yet combed, she was wearing what was called a bungalow apron, and she looked a mess. Her sister Alta was there with her but refused to go to the door, so Lila had no choice but to do it. He was selling Accident and Health Insurance, which she told him she did not need. But he was a good salesman, and had answers for each of her excuses. His insurance would be good anywhere in the U.S., to which she replied "After this year, I'll be going out of the country as a missionary." It turned out that he, too, was a Student Volunteer planning to be a missionary, and he was working his way through medical school by selling insurance. Needless to say, she eventually took a policy.

Having sold the policy, he asked if he could come back and call on her that evening. She agreed, and a neighbor took them out for a long drive.

A few days later, Lila was leaving for St. Paul, Minnesota, to visit a dear friend who had recently moved to Minnesota from South Dakota. This was a woman in whose home Lila had worked when she was in college. On her way to the train, she stopped at the post office and found a letter from the insurance salesman, Royce Engberg, a student at Northwestern University Medical School.

When Lila showed his letter to her friend in St. Paul and told her the story behind it, her friend said, "You can marry him any time you're ready to say the word." Lila was sure she knew better. Eventually she answered his letter, and over time, they became acquainted by mail.

Lila was still teaching in Webster, and on her birthday in October, she received a 40" box containing nine huge, beautiful yellow chrysanthemums. It was the first time she had ever received a gift of flowers, and she was flabbergasted. The people in that small town were pretty flabbergasted, too, because, of course, the grape vine carried the news to everyone.

Soon Lila and Royce were writing to each other every day. At Christmas time, when she went to St. Paul again, he came there to see her over New Year's and they became engaged. It was only the second time they had seen each other. Lila wrote to the Woman's Foreign Missionary Society and told them her news. She also told them that her husband-to-be was studying to be a medical missionary, and they released her with their blessing.

Lila and Royce were married on August 22, 1922, in St. Paul, Minnesota, and then moved to Chicago where Royce was a senior in medical school. They lived at 2121 South Lawndale Avenue in Chicago. They took in a roomer, Livonia Defore, to help with the rent. Lila taught English at Cicero, Illinois that year and their daughter, Mildred, was born on January 5, 1924, at Chicago's Lutheran Memorial Hospital. Mildred called Livonia "Donie" because she couldn't say "Livonia".

Lila and Royce were determined to be good parents, and they had their own ideas about what that meant. For one thing, Mildred would learn to call things by their proper names, so she early learned, and tried to say, that her belly button was her umbilicus. Those who took care of her, Lila's sister Alta or Livonia, knew what she meant when she told them she needed to have a bow-moonut (bowel movement) and they would take her to her potty chair.

Lila and Royce eventually bought a highchair for Mildred. When they put her in it for the first time, Mildred looked back and forth between them, as they watched expectantly to see her reaction. Since her only "chair" up to that time had been her potty chair, she proceeded to "grunt" as she had been taught to do when put on the potty chair.

One evening in the fall of 1924, Lila and Royce went out and left Mildred at home alone with Alta, who was spending a few days with them before leaving for India. Alta had been warned not to pick up the baby if she cried; let her cry and she'd settle down. Needless to say, they had not been gone very long when Mildred did cry. She cried and cried and cried. Finally, Alta could stand it no longer so she tiptoed in to see what was the matter. Poor little Mildred had thrown up her supper. She was lying on her back and what Alta called "the nasty stuff" was all over her little face and she was a pitiful sight. So Alta picked her up, washed her face, gave her a clean nightgown, and tried to put her to bed again. But it was no use. Mildred did not want to sleep. So Alta put her in her high chair and played with her, and that's where they were when Lila and Royce came home. Lila was very cross with her and Alta felt that Lila didn't really believe her story.

Lila and Royce had also decided that they would not talk about their baby all the time, the way most new parents of their acquaintance did. So they never mentioned Mildred unless someone asked about her. One evening they were entertaining a young couple whom they knew quite well. The young woman asked if they could see the baby. Lila said, "Of course," and went to get her. When she returned the young woman was obviously surprised. She explained that because neither Lila nor Royce had ever talked about Mildred, they were sure the baby had some serious deformity.

Royce finished medical school in June of 1924 and was accepted at Cook County Hospital where he started his 18-month internship on January 1, 1925. Cook County Hospital was, at that time, the first choice for many interns. It was always a very busy place and Royce was enthusiastic about his work, always going the extra mile. That year there was a serious flu epidemic, with many cases going into pneumonia, but Royce never tried to save himself. On March 21, he went home with a high fever. He was later taken back to the hospital where he died of double pneumonia on April 1, 1925, after only three months of his internship.

When Lila came home from the hospital after Royce died, Mildred cried when Lila opened the door. She had always slept soundly before. From the time she was born, Mildred had never been a cuddly baby and often straightened out stiff when Lila or Royce tried to cuddle her. That night, when Lila came in, she cuddled for the first time. When Royce died, Mildred became Lila's reason for being.

An obituary in the *Chicago Herald Examiner*, commenting on Royce's ambition to be a missionary and the loss sustained by his passing, said: "Out at (Cook) County Hospital, suffering and death are familiar things. They are the routine of daily existence. But yesterday they came poignantly to that great building and saddened it. Dr. Royce Engberg died. His name may not seem familiar to newspaper readers because he was only 27 and just starting on the road that his colleagues said would inevitably lead to fame...Ten days ago he collapsed...a victim of double pneumonia. There was scarcely an eminent physician on the staff who did not ask to attend him. There was not an intern who failed to offer his help. But Dr. Frederick Tice, one of the best known physicians in the country, insisted that he be allowed to handle the case..."

The newspaper obituary in Odebolt, Iowa, where Royce had been born and raised, was 25" long. It began: "'Death is a Hard Master' and 'Death Loves a Shining Mark.' These phrases are surely most applicable at this time in reporting the passing of one of our noblest and best young men, Dr. Royce Raymond Engberg, who died in Chicago, after but a short but serious illness, double pneumonia…His future full of promise, and we dare not ask why he was taken from us in his prime, unless, as flowers are picked before the frost finds them, that we may not witness their decay." It went on to quote extensively from the obituary that had been in the *Herald Examiner*, and listed the many friends and relatives who had attended the funeral which was held in Odebolt, Iowa.

Lila closed up their apartment in Chicago, sold their furnishings, and she and Mildred went to Mitchell, South Dakota, to stay with her sister Elsie and her husband, Fred Rolfe, till she knew what would be next.

Lila & Mildred, 1926

TO INDIA

After closing the apartment in Chicago, Lila returned to Mitchell, South Dakota, to stay with her sister and her husband, Elsie and Fred Rolfe. Both Elsie and Fred worked in a local florist, so Lila took care of Mildred and kept house for them. They had a small home and they raised a few chickens and had a small garden. Lila kept hoping and praying that she would be able to go to India, where she could take care of her baby and earn her living as a missionary.

Meantime, their sister Alta had gone to India in 1924 to manage a girls' school in Lahore in what is now Pakistan. Alta had also studied at Dakota Wesleyan University and had signed up to be a missionary so she could travel. After Royce died, Lila was distraught. She wrote pathetic letters to Alta telling how upset she was, how she was suffering with boils that made her really ill. During the summer of 1925, Alta went to the mountains for her vacation, and had a chance to talk with the India-Secretary of the Woman's Foreign Missionary Society (WFMS) about Lila and the fact that she wanted to go to India. The president of Lila's alma mater, Dakota Wesleyan University, Dr. Schermerhorn, had also been a missionary in India, and he, too, was trying to help her.

Suddenly, through the combined efforts of Lila, Alta in India, and Dr. Schermerhorn in South Dakota, Lila was told that there was a place for her to teach in an English boarding school in Darjeeling, up in the Himalaya mountains. This was 1925, so it took a month for the letter to reach her from India and another month for her reply to reach them, but Lila was exuberant when she learned that she might go.

But there were still hurdles. "Send a widow and baby to India?" The WFMS knew they were taking a chance. Arrangements were made for Lila and Mildred to have physical examinations in Minneapolis, since it was from that branch of the WFMS that she would be sent out. Lila knew she was not in her best physical condition, and, when the physician hesitated and then asked if she really wanted to go to India, she broke down and cried. He had found a slight heart murmur and that was why he was hesitating, but when he saw that she was really anxious to go, he passed her.

Friends and relatives in the U.S. thought she was crazy to take Mildred to heathen India. They predicted all sorts of dire consequences, but Lila believed that it was God's will and that He would give her the strength she would need. One relative told her point blank that it was stupid or worse, and that if anything ever happened to Mildred, it would be Lila's own fault. She never forgot those words.

She signed a three-year contract with the Woman's Foreign Missionary Society of the Methodist Church, and on January 1, 1926, Lila and Mildred set sail from New York on the S.S. Homeric. Mildred had her second birthday on the Atlantic (Incidentally, she had her seventh birthday on the Pacific in 1931, when they were returning to India after a six-month furlough in the U.S.) It was a rough crossing, and nearly everyone was seasick, but not Lila. She would put the two-year-old Mildred on the floor and as the ship rolled back and forth, Mildred would roll from one side of the room to the other. They were traveling with another missionary family all of whom were ill all the way to Cherbourg. From Cherbourg, they crossed Europe and took another ship from Marseilles to Bombay via the Suez Canal.

Although Alta was already living in India, she didn't know Lila was on her way until she received Lila's cable from Port Said. Immediately, she sent off a letter which was awaiting Lila's arrival in Bombay the end of January. There, Lila and Mildred stayed at the Methodist Mission, while they cleared customs and made arrangements to join Alta in Lahore until school opened the beginning of March.

From Lahore, they went to Arrah, in Bihar province, to visit another missionary friend who was also a graduate of Dakota Wesleyan. That evening at dinner, Lila asked about the humming sound she heard. "Mosquitoes!" she was told. Right after dinner, she and Mildred went to bed—in a single bed. Lila had never seen a mosquito net, so she didn't know that one must tuck them in on all four sides of the bed. Toward morning, she was wakened by Mildred's restlessness. It was getting light, so she sat up and saw that the inside of the net was black with mosquitoes. Mildred looked like she had the measles; she was covered with mosquito bites! Lila drew a circle the size of a dime on her own knuckle and counted 64 bites within the circle. She was tough, so her bites dried up and faded away pretty soon. Mildred's became infected and she got malaria, which Lila had to fight periodically over the next few years. Eventually, she read about Esanophele tablets, which she bought, and after the first few, Mildred's malaria left her and she never had another attack. [During World War II, Mildred tried to donate blood but was refused as a donor because she had had malaria.]

They took the train from Arrah to Calcutta. In order to be thrifty, Lila took third class, not knowing anything about the conditions in which they would be traveling. The train was noisy, crowded, and dirty, but they finally reached Calcutta, having picked up head lice on the way. Before lunch the first day at the mission house in Calcutta, Lila washed Mildred's hair with a suggested treatment for the lice, and they went down to lunch with Mildred's hair bundled in a towel. One of the other missionaries at the lunch table commented "Did the little girl have her hair washed?" to which Mildred responded gaily, "Yes. I have lice!" To treat her own case of head lice, Lila sprayed her head with Flit, a common treatment for all sorts of household vermin in those days. The Flit killed the lice, but it also caused her hair to fall out in handfuls.

The trip from Calcutta to Darjeeling was another unique experience. They took trains north to reach Darjeeling. They left Calcutta late in the afternoon on a regular wide gauge train, changed in the night to a medium gauge train, and, in the morning, got into a rear car on the Darjeeling Himalayan Railway, the so-called Toy Train, because it runs on a narrow 24" gauge. The train winds around the mountains, sometimes backing up to go higher and higher and often positioned so that the front of the train overlapped the rear. There were no restrooms on the train, and there came a time when two-year-old Mildred needed one. Since there was no alternative, Lila held her out the train window to do what was necessary. It happened to be at one of the times when the front of the train overlapped the rear of the train as it circled the mountain, so everyone on the train was able to see what was going on. After a six-hour ride, they arrived in bitter cold Darjeeling. Miss Stahl, the principal of the school where Lila was to teach, met them at the station, took one look at Mildred, and said, "What has she got?" Mosquito bites.

Later, Lila understood her concern. Miss Stahl was the principal of a boarding school, Queens Hill, where the children lived in close proximity to each other in dormitories, so any contagious disease was a serious threat. They ate in a common dining room and they were always together. There was a full-time nurse on the staff, and the English Civil Surgeon was always on call from Darjeeling. In fact, he came to the school every Monday morning to provide routine medical care.

In India, Mildred lived through pneumonia twice, flu, tonsillitis, whooping cough, malaria, and epidemics of measles, chicken pox, and mumps. She started whooping with the whooping cough while she was on the operating table having her tonsils removed. The one epidemic that Mildred avoided was diphtheria. To avoid that, she had been given an anti-toxin to which it turned out she was allergic. She developed a rash that was only relieved by the continuous application of compresses of witch hazel and baking soda. Lila often wondered if it would have been better for her to get diphtheria, since the treatment of the rash lasted for weeks. One long-term benefit of Mildred's many illnesses was that she learned to knit while she was confined, a hobby that she continued to enjoy for the rest of her life.

Lila's first job in Darjeeling, before school started, was to engage an ayah to take care of Mildred while she was teaching and on duty. Lila had talked to Mildred every day about Darjeeling and what she would be doing, and how there would be an ayah to be with her all the time when Lila was working. Every time Mildred saw an Indian woman, she would ask, "Is this my ayah?" until it became embarrassing. They all wanted to be her ayah.

Lila talked with Miss Stahl, the principal, about getting an ayah who would be clean, competent, and dependable. Finally, Miss Stahl picked out the small Nepalese wife of one of the school servants. She was clean and very bright, had children of her own, and she loved Mildred. Almost over night, she learned to understand Mildred, and soon Mildred was speaking Nepalese and serving as Lila's interpreter. One day, Lila told Mildred to ask the ayah something. They conversed and went back to their play. When Lila asked Mildred what the ayah had said, Mildred replied, "You heard her."

When they first went to Darjeeling, Mildred never saw any men except the Indian servants. One day, she heard a man's voice in the hall and she went running to Lila and slammed the door behind her, screaming, "Mummy, a man, a man!" Seeing that she was afraid of men, Lila cultivated married friends and also managed to have Mildred spend a few weeks of every year in a normal home away from her mother.

Although Lila had been sent to Darjeeling as a "Contract Teacher" for a three-year term, she stayed four years. In a boarding school, a missionary teacher is on duty 24 hours a day, seven days a week. Her specific responsibilities included being in charge of the older girls' dormitory, which was next to the room that she and Mildred shared. She also conducted morning worship services; took her turn at various duties, such as supervision in study halls and dining rooms; and taught English, Scripture, Algebra, and other subjects.

Queen's Hill School was primarily for the children of missionaries and other Europeans, as most white people were called. The students were taught a British curriculum, which prepared them to take Junior and Senior Cambridge Examinations, sent out from England. These examinations were administered each December following the end of the school year, which ran from March through November. One year, Lila discovered at the end of the year that one of the classes preparing for the Cambridge Examinations had not been taught by the correct syllabus in their Scripture course. With only two weeks until the examination, she taught the students what they were supposed to have learned during the year, and not one of them failed the examination.

The school was also associated with The Associated Board of the Royal Schools of Music in London, which sent examiners to evaluate the music achievement of individual students seeking their certification. Mildred took piano lessons at the school from the age of four, and took the associated examinations the last two years that they lived in India.

The credentials provided by the two aforementioned institutions were accepted world-wide when the students returned to their home countries.

When Lila and Mildred first arrived in Darjeeling, Mildred was in the habit of calling her mother by her first name. After all, everyone who knew her called her "Lila." But many of the other missionaries thought it was highly inappropriate for a 2-year-old to call her mother by her first name. So Lila sat down with Mildred and explained the situation to her. Most of the other children in the school called their mothers "Mummy" so Lila suggested Mildred adopt that practice. During the transition, Mildred used "Mummy-Lila" but eventually she grew comfortable calling Lila "Mummy".

Other teachers would sometimes ask Lila to wake them in the morning so they would be on time for classes. So Lila would send Mildred on the errand with instructions to tell the teacher it was half-past-seven. Mildred could then be heard going down the hall from Lila's room to the teacher's room, chanting all the way, "Mummy says it's half-past-seven, Mummy says it's half-past-seven."

Being in charge of the older girls' dormitory also meant meting out discipline when it was needed. On one occasion, Lila was summoned because one of the girls had "fainted." When Lila arrived on the scene, she was told that the girl, who was lying on the floor, often fainted. After hearing the other girls' explanation of the situation, Lila asked someone to bring a glass of water, which she calmly poured on the girl's face. For some reason, the girl never fainted again.

One time, the girls were eating tinned fruits in the dormitory and got sticky syrup all over the floor. When Lila came into the room, she stepped into it. She sent one of the girls to get a pail of water and another to get a supply of rags. Then she had the girls wash the floor.

Other examples of discipline were equally colorful. When students had been flicking spoonfuls of water at each other in the dining room, Lila had them come out to the playground after the meal wearing their raincoats. Each of the guilty students was given a teaspoon and a pitcher of water, with instructions to stand there and flick the water at each other.

In a similar vein, in a study hall that Lila was supervising, some students were whispering instead of studying for an upcoming examination. Lila took their books away from them and wouldn't let them study. She soon got a reputation as being a firm but fair disciplinarian and she rarely had problems with the students.

The year 1926, when Lila arrived in Darjeeling, was the year that Queen's Hill School moved to the Mount Hermon estate. The school was in a brand new fieldstone, three-story building with a basement which housed the kitchen and a large area used for a variety of activities. The previous school building had been nearer to the city of Darjeeling, but it had been destroyed, with much loss of life, in a landslide.

The year 1926 was also the first year of co-education at Queen's Hill. Up to that time, only small boys under the age of ten had been accepted; above that age, they went to a boys' school. Most of the teachers were Anglo-Indians, and Lila was the only person on the staff who had ever taught boys before. As a result, she had the older boys in her home room and she was responsible for their discipline. The boys were American, English, and Anglo-Indian. The boys soon got to know Lila.

As an illustration, one day the boys, aged 13 and 14, did something for which they had to be punished. They were turned over to Lila. When she dismissed the other children from the dining room after tiffin (a light meal served at 3 p.m.), Lila asked the boys to stay. As she talked with them, they admitted that they had to be punished, "But none of that girl stuff!" they said. "OK, so what shall your punishment be?" she asked. "Cane us!" came the reply, almost defiantly. Lila agreed and told them to go out and bring their switches but they'd have to tell her how to do it. When they returned, they bent over, hands clasping their ankles, and said, "Do it hard!" So she did it "hard" till they told her to stop. Then they shook hands and thanked her. Thereafter, they could face the boys in the All-Boys schools and brag about having been caned.

Another time, one of the small American boys had been sent to Lila's office to be punished. She asked him what kind of punishment he thought she should give him, and he asked for a spanking. So she bent him over her knee and spanked him, after which he climbed into her lap, put his arms around her neck, and said, "Thank you, Mrs. Engberg."

Students in one class had been cheating, and someone tattled to the teacher, Mrs. Ryan. Mrs. Ryan was very strict and stern so the students expected severe punishment when she came to class. As a prank, they all had reversed tangerine skins covering their teeth. When Mrs. Ryan saw them, she stormed out of the room and went to get Lila. Lila came to the class and asked for their side of the story. Then she made them promise never to cheat again, and she would deal with Mrs. Ryan.

What the students had no way of knowing was that Mrs. Ryan hated teaching. She had gotten married to get out of it. She had a child, but her husband and child were both killed in a boating accident. She had had to resume teaching to support herself. Lila tried to work with her and help her to deal with her personal situation.

Since the school had a kindergarten, Mildred started attending it right away and continued for the next four years. She loved school and, despite being sick much of the time, she progressed. She was able to read when she was three years old and could write her name when she was four. The kindergarten taught much of what American children were learning in the first two grades.

As already noted, during Alta's fourth year in Lahore, she was sent to Ajmer to fill a vacancy there. In Ajmer, she met Cecil Harris to whom she became engaged after a year, and married early in 1930. Lila and Mildred were present for the wedding, with Mildred serving as flower girl.

Soon after the wedding, in January 1930, after four happy years in Darjeeling, Lila and Mildred left India for a furlough in America. On the trip, they were accompanied by Miss Stahl, the retiring principal of the school. The three of them shared a cabin on a lower deck. When the ship was passing through the Red Sea, the sea was rough and Miss Stahl had the berth under the porthole. A wave poured through the open porthole bringing live fish and drenching Miss Stahl and all her belongings, which she had left on the floor.

While sight-seeing in Egypt, Lila was spat upon. She asked the guide if he understood what had happened. His response was, "They thought you were Jewish." The travelers also visited other countries in northern Africa and Europe on their way home, with Mildred and Lila compiling scrapbooks of the sites they visited

In the U.S., Lila was occupied with traveling for the WFMS, telling church groups about mission work in India and throughout the world. She left Mildred with her friends in Minnesota, and Mildred went to school there for four months. Initially, when Lila took Mildred to enroll her in the school, because Mildred was six years old, the school wanted to put her in first grade. Lila would have none of that. So they said they would try Mildred in second grade. After a few days of that, the school decided she was too far advanced to stay in the second grade, so they put her in the third grade, which was a bit more difficult but still not challenging enough to keep her occupied. Finally, she was put in the fourth grade, to the dismay of the principal who could not condone having a 6-year-old in the 4ᵗʰ grade. But Mildred worked hard and did reasonably well.

It was in Minnesota that Mildred first learned to trust dogs. The friend with whom they were staying had a black cocker spaniel called "Nigger". Nigger would escort Mildred to school and then return to escort her home at the end of the day. He would sleep on the foot of her bed, but when he heard Lila coming to bed, he would get off Mildred's bed and hide underneath till Lila had settled down. From that point on, Mildred never had a fear of dogs.

Lila and Mildred had been in the U.S. less than a year when Lila received a cable asking her to return as the principal of Queens Hill School. They returned in early 1931. As principal, Lila had a suite of rooms on the third floor of the school building, with windows looking north toward the Kinchenjunga range. Mildred shared her rooms, until 1934, when she was 10 years old and moved into the girls' dormitory. Lila's suite consisted of four rooms: a living room, bedroom, bathroom, and sewing room. In the living room, there was a fireplace, and the cement floor was covered with her 9' x 12' Chinese rug. In the sewing room, she had her electric sewing machine, which she had brought from America, and her American electric iron. She also had an American electric waffle iron. To use these appliances, she had a transformer, since Indian electric outlets did not accommodate the American plugs.

Lila often entertained visiting dignitaries for tea in her living quarters. On such occasions, she would usually have a fire in the fireplace, and serve Darjeeling tea, accompanied by waffles. The waffles were sometimes flavored with cheese or chocolate, but even ordinary waffles were an unfamiliar treat for anyone in India.

Lila used her sewing machine to make many of her own clothes and all of Mildred's clothes, except for school uniforms. Even after they returned to America, and when Mildred went away to college and then married, Lila continued to make clothes for her.

Lila's position as principal of the school was a very responsible position with a good deal of authority, and Lila very much enjoyed it. She lacked self-confidence but she loved the feeling of power. She liked being able to do things to make the school and its pupils grow and develop. She was happy in her work and would have been content to live there the rest of her days. She was quite popular; she had a position of respect and responsibility, and she felt that she did her work well; the teachers, pupils, and parents all cooperated and the future looked bright.

Then, in January 1934, the earthquake struck and everything changed.

EARTHQUAKE

Lila and Mildred were in Calcutta on January 15, 1934 taking their usual afternoon rest when there was a major earthquake in India. In Calcutta it lasted for eight minutes. They followed the usual evacuation procedures, which meant going outdoors and leaning against the building. The theory was that if anything fell off the building, it was not likely to fall straight down.

The next day, the newspapers were full of the news of the earthquake. There were places where the earth had opened up and people had fallen in. Buildings had collapsed, crushing people to death. People were sleeping in the parks because they feared more tremors. The damage in the Himalayas nearer the epicenter had been even more severe, although it had been felt for little more than a minute.

Lila received a telegram from Darjeeling, which read: "School extensively damaged. Come immediately." So she went, leaving Mildred with missionaries in Calcutta. School was scheduled to open the first week of March. Was the school going to be usable? What would she do? What could she do?

Queen's Hill School was built in the shape of a large U, with a quadrangle play-ground between the two wings. In one wing of the U there was the Assembly Hall, which was two stories high, and below it the Kindergarten. The other wing was three stories high with teachers' rooms on the top floor, dormitories on the second floor, and classrooms on the first floor. Both wings had been virtually destroyed and all of the interior partitions in the building had fallen like blocks. There were six weeks in which to get the place habitable before school was to have opened.

The school was already in debt and the managing committee said they could not afford to rebuild it because it was estimated that it would cost $35,000, a lot of money in India at any time and certainly in 1934. Lila insisted that the school had to be rebuilt and that they would get the money somehow. That was the beginning of a year that was a nightmare for Lila.

School opened only 10 days later than had been planned. It was exactly two months to the day since the earthquake, but all the partitions were in. Work continued on the outside walls until August. Lila had made friends and had a good reputation among Indian government officials who thought highly of her ability and her efficiency. She used her connections to get a substantial amount of earthquake relief money to rebuild the school.

Meantime, what about the students who were going to attend the school? They had seen newspaper stories of damage in Darjeeling, so they wondered what would happen to them. Little by little, word spread among the students that Lila had been summoned and that the school was seriously damaged. Eventually, Lila was able to send letters to all the students' families describing the situation she had found and the plans as she saw them. She said that the school had been judged to be structurally sound and it was expected that it could be repaired sufficiently to open it but a bit later than originally planned.

Some parents were worried about sending their children up to Darjeeling, so they took a trip up to see for themselves. They returned to tell others how all the partition walls in the two upper stories had been dismantled where the living quarters were located, and they were being rebuilt with reinforced concrete, so the building would be quite new and entirely safe. Until the building was done, the staff would live in cottages on the school grounds that were usually occupied by parents visiting their children during the school year.

When the students arrived on March 15th, there were piles of stones; mounds of broken plaster, sand, and other debris; a forest of scaffoldings; the broken ends of the school's two wings; hundreds of broken windows; bent and twisted steel girders. Many saw it as a picture of desolation and destruction. Inside, the building reeked of new paint, new plaster, and varnish. It was cold and damp. The floors were not their usual spotlessly clean. There was evidence of fresh cement everywhere. The building looked quite safe, but very depressing.

Some students tried surreptitiously to make arrangements to go back to their homes. Others stood rooted to the spot, not knowing how they could adjust to what stood before them. Some went directly to Lila and asked her to let them go home at once. Lila gave each of them her time and attention and asked them to try it for two weeks. If, at the end of two weeks, they still wanted to go home, she would make the arrangements. Apparently, it worked. No one went home.

School was organized and classes began immediately. They were held wherever space could be found: in the library, an unoccupied office, the sewing room, the art room, anywhere. Two dormitories had been destroyed, so sleeping arrangements were created by crowding beds into the usable dormitories. The next morning, the bell rang as usual for students to attend morning prayers—but the Assembly Hall had been destroyed. They were crowded into what had been the teachers' parlor, where benches had been placed. Everyone had a seat, but their knees were up to their chins and they looked like a tin of sardines.

That temporary arrangement proved to be unsatisfactory so after a couple of weeks, a divider curtain was hung in the children's dining room and the benches were put there for church and chapel services. The arrangements made the dining tables very close together causing problems for the bearers serving food, but it was manageable.

Classes began in earnest despite the pounding, coolies singing, chipping stones, etc. Teachers developed strong lungs in order to be heard above the din. Daily the work continued, and daily everyone watched the progress. When the children had arrived on March 15th, the Assembly Hall and Kindergarten wing had already been dismantled, the roof was off, the walls had been torn down to the foundation, and they were already rebuilding. They were still dismantling the classroom and dormitory wing. Day by day, the reconstruction progressed.

It was a tradition at the school to hold an annual Sale Day in May. To this event, parents and other guests were invited. There were speeches, entertainment, and concerts. In 1934, Sale Day was held on Saturday, May 26. The Assembly Hall, though still incomplete, was used for the first time, despite the fact that it resembled a huge barn with a tin roof.

Soon after Sale Day, the Kindergarten was able to move down to their old quarters. Gradually, the hammering, pounding, and scraping diminished. The scaffolding was removed from the exterior and the finishing touches commenced. Now, in place of the sand and debris on the playgrounds, there were resurfaced tennis courts, new swings, and new playground equipment. The Assembly Hall had a big beautiful stage in place of the inadequate one of the past. The acoustics of the hall had been improved by the installation of a special ceiling and stage. The exterior, too, was more imposing, with the seal of the school at the top gable and the name "Mount Hermon School" across the end of the wing where it could be seen as one approached the school.

A word about the name of the school. When it opened in 1926, it had the same name as its predecessor, Queen's Hill School. It was built on land known as the Mount Hermon Estate. Over the years, as the number of male students increased, many of them expressed their disapproval of the name "Queen's Hill School". It sounded sissy. Gradually, the name "Mount Hermon School" had crept into general usage. So when the school was rebuilt, the name was officially changed to Mount Hermon and that name was emblazoned on the end of one wing.

During the 1934 school year, Lila arranged for the publication and distribution of a little booklet (3½ x 4¾") entitled "What is an Educated Heart?" In January of that year, the *Reader's Digest* magazine had printed an article, "The Educated Heart" by Gillett Burgess, from which the booklet was developed. The Preface, signed by Lila, said: "This little booklet is presented to you in order to help you to lay solid foundations for Christian Characters. I hope it will help you to form good habits, attitudes and relationships in the life and work of the school, and in your later life. Remember, boys and girls, that the only human example we have of a Perfect Educated Heart is found in our Bible. I would urge each of you to take Jesus as your example and try to develop an Educated Heart." Each page of the booklet presented a set of rules and a familiar quotation related to one of the following characteristics of an Educated Heart:: Reverence, Loyalty, Truth, Social Attitudes, Obedience, Punctuality, Stick-To-It-Iveness, Self-control, Initiative, Judgment, Thrift, and Good Sportsmanship. Throughout the year, Chapel services addressed the various rules and their application in students' lives.

As principal of the school, Lila made it a practice to send letters to the parents of the children periodically. One of those letters was dated July 27, 1934. It is reprinted here because it reveals something of Lila's responsibilities and practices as principal of that mission school at that time in its history:

Dear Parents:

I have had several inquiries about our date for going down this year. The school party will leave here on Monday, Dec. 3ʳᵈ. That is exactly ten days later than the date I had asked for before the earthquake, but we came up just ten days later also.

A couple months ago I mentioned in my letter that we are making arrangements for a more adequate school uniform for next year. Whiteaway Laidlaw have now in stock boys' hose sizes 7½ to 10½ for Rs. 2/- to Rs. 2/12 per pair. These are wool hose with the gold double border below the knee. Caps are Rs. 2/3 each; elastic web blue and gold belts with a snake fastener @ 1/3; little girls' hose sizes 6 to 10 @ 1/8 to Rs. 2/per pair. If you wish us to get these things for your children, write and we shall give the order. I am getting prices of tennis socks with a gold border for the bigger girls to wear.

I am making a campaign against our children reading trashy literature. I wish to make an appeal to you parents not to send the girls and boys any magazines except really good literature. I am forbidding them spending time reading Movie magazines etc. They can put their time to much better use than filling

their heads full of trashy reading and I'm sure you all agree with me and coop-
erate.

We have begun our special study of Ideals or Character Traits for this year. Each
pupil is given a pamphlet "What is an Educated Heart?" This booklet has the
rules for developing an Educated Heart or for forming a Christian Character.
Last year we started this study and it was so successful and was spoken of so
highly by both pupils and teachers that we decided to elaborate on the rules
and to try to make them apply more closely to our own school. We have based
the study upon an article in the Readers' Digest, "The Educated Heart." This
article has proved so helpful to pupils and teachers that we decided to weave
our own traits around this and make our finished product an "Educated Heart."
I hope you will remember to ask your children about the pamphlet when they
come home and will try to continue the training through the holidays.

In case you are planning a trip to Darjeeling this autumn, I am giving the dates
of some of the coming events in the school so you might time your coming for
some of these. Each fortnight we have a recital by the piano pupils. We had one
a fortnight ago, and one Friday the 27th of this month. Work has begun on the
recitation contests. There will be six preliminary contests (dates will be settled
later) and then the final contest will be held on October 30th.

Miss Sutton has done some very good work in her Drill Classes this year and she
is having them give a Gym Display on September 28th. We have set October 6th
for our Sports' Day. On October 10th, we are having a School Sale, Tea, and
Concert. The Concert is to be an Operetta by the Junior Singing Class. The Trin-
ity College Music Exams are to be September 24th or 26th; Associated Board
Exams October 23–25. The Progress Association is having its annual Floral Fete
on October 20th and our school will give an item on the programme. The Euro-
pean Schools' Singing Festival is to be on Nov. 10th, I hear.

The staff is very busy getting the Blue and Gold ready for publication. We shall
hear more about that later.

Almost everybody in the school has had mumps now so the epidemic is subsid-
ing. We have had over 70 cases in all not counting the day scholars who have
had it. Our Isolation hospital is without any occupants at present for the first
time since the last of March. We are not sorry.

I'm sure you will be very sad to hear that Mr. Sur's daughter, who I told you had
galloping consumption, passed away in Calcutta on July 12th. Mr. Sur will soon
be back here in the office, and Miss Field has come up from her work in Calcutta for a couple weeks and I am to go away for a two weeks' rest. I shall be in
the station near enough to be called in case of an emergency.

Before another month has gone we expect to be in the whole of our repaired
sections of the building. We are now using the classrooms and teachers' rooms.
The dorms will be completed in another few days and the assembly hall in a

couple of weeks. We hope to have an opening of the new wings in the autumn when Government is up here, especially if they give us a substantial grant towards these repairs!

Yours sincerely,

L. Engberg

Seven months to the day after the earthquake, on August 15th, the new Assembly Hall was re-dedicated. To quote from the dedicatory speech: "We need not mourn for the greater glory of the former building that was shattered by the earthquake. Instead we all rejoice that the latter glory is greater than the former. The Assembly Hall is now more firmly constructed, more strongly bound together than before. We would now, therefore, render hearts full of thanksgiving to our Gracious God who, of his infinite mercy and goodness, has made all this possible. It was He who gave the faith and courage that enabled us to say: 'It shall be rebuilt!'"

So the school was rebuilt; it was well regarded by the parents and by the Indian government; the children were happy. It seemed that what Lila had done had turned out well. But the building committee and the people in charge in the mission were displeased. Lila's success in raising the money and getting the school rebuilt, when they had thought it couldn't be done, did not please them. They wanted to get rid of her, so when her four-year contract expired, they refused to renew it. Lila had given what she considered nine of the best years of her life to the school and she had loved it. She believed she had done her work well, that she had many friends and few enemies, but the enemies had the real power.

School closed in December, so Lila and Mildred left India later that winter. On their way back to the United States, they stopped in England and spent three months with Alta, Cecil, and their two children, Lenore, born in 1930, and Alfred, born in 1933. Mildred attended school in London during the time they were there.

In May, 1935, Lila and Mildred sailed from Southampton to New York on Cunard's Berengaria.

BACK IN THE U.S.

Although Lila had taken six extension courses from the University of Chicago while she was in India, she did not feel equal to the competition in the U.S. People returning to India after furlough in the States had reported that there were 20 people for every job. After all, it was 1935, the depth of the Depression. So she decided she must go to graduate school.

Lila started her graduate work at Northwestern University in Evanston, Illinois, in the summer session of 1935. Her reports say that she had four objectives: (1) to get to know America again, its new social and economic problems and the New Social Order; (2) to prepare herself to get a job, since she was told that her experience had been the wrong kind and she would have to compete with those much younger than herself; (3) to see first hand what was going on in the world of education; and (4) to find a niche that she could fill with an opportunity to do some kind of satisfying work.

That first summer was a period of adjustment, without guidance. Lila felt ignorant. The professors used terminology she did not understand. She spent days and nights at the library, reading everything she could find. There was so much she didn't know. There was so little plan or purpose to her choice of courses and to her reading. There seemed no one to guide her. Everyone seemed so busy, in contrast with the leisurely pace of the Orient. At this time, she was not interested in getting a degree, and everyone else was working on degrees. She just wanted to belong, to readjust to this new busy America.

To take stock of her ability and her liabilities, Lila was persuaded to go to the Graduate Teachers College in Winnetka, Illinois that fall. She had been hearing about this new "Progressive Education" and Dr. Washburne seemed to be the incarnation of whatever that was. She spent a semester there and learned that was not what she wanted.

Simultaneously with her work in Winnetka, Lila was taking some courses on the campus at Northwestern University. She was also the house mother in one of the women's dormitories, and Mildred shared an apartment with her while attending 8th grade at Haven School in Evanston. At Northwestern University,

Lila began seriously to work in the field of guidance. Her goals now became to get a Master's degree and a satisfying job.

In Lila's studies her focus gradually shifted from the curriculum and subject-matter to a study of the whole child—individual differences; physical, social, mental and emotional growth; methods of guidance; adjusting the school to the child. She worked with many leaders in the field of Education at Northwestern University and got to know some of them very well. This provided one of the greatest joys in her graduate work, because it allowed her to know the personalities behind many of the books and articles she had been reading.

After the year of graduate work at Northwestern University, Lila needed to get a full-time job. She wanted to continue her education, but she had to face reality. Mildred was 12 years old and entering 9th grade. So, when Lila learned of a position teaching in a Methodist Girls' High School, she applied, thinking that Mildred could attend the school, too. Lila was interviewed by the school's president, Dr. Wright.

During the course of the interview, Lila asked Dr. Wright if the girls in the school had any contact with boys. After all, she had taken a course in adolescent psychology, and she knew a few things about teen-aged girls. "Oh, yes," he assured her. "Once a year there's a dance to which the boys at a nearby boys' school are invited."

At another point in the interview, Dr. Wright interrupted their conversation to suggest that he would prefer that she not wear lipstick. She always wore Tangee lipstick, a brand that was barely visible lip-coloring.

Lila began to understand why it was called "Drew Seminary for Young Women.": Later she learned that the girls in the school called it the "Drew Cemetery for Young Corpses." But she needed the job, so she took it. She taught Ancient History, Mental Hygiene, and other subjects, and she also took some courses at Columbia University that year. Mildred, who had always hated History and had done very poorly in it, loved Lila's Ancient History. Lila gave her 98 on the final exam because Mildred was her daughter, although she later told Mildred that any other child in the class would have gotten 100 for the same exam.

Lila had always made Mildred's clothes, but at Drew, all the girls wore Kelly green blouses over skirts of the same color, with forest green pussy-cat bows tied under the collar. They also wore long, thick, dark lisle stockings and black shoes. Lila still liked to sew, and she would sit on the floor to cut out the patterns, often whistling to herself as she worked. One evening, as she sat on the floor working, there was a knock on her door. When she called "Come in," the Dean of Women, Miss Russell, entered.

"Mrs. Engberg," she said. "Did you hear someone whistling?"

"No, Miss Russell," she lied.

"Well, you know," Miss Russell continued, "young ladies never whistle."

Miss Russell was a very strict Dean of Women. She made rules, and the girls were expected to obey them. For example, if the girls took a walk into the town of Carmel, NY (population 900, at that time), at least three of them were to walk together, for their safety. And if, by chance, they were in danger of encountering a male individual on the sidewalk, they were to cross the street and walk on the other side.

Another extreme example of Miss Russell's suspicious nature came one night when she knocked on the door of a room occupied by two girls, Frances and Darlene. Since Miss Russell often prowled the halls and called on the girls toward bedtime, perhaps checking to be sure they hadn't sneaked out, they were not really surprised. But what Miss Russell said in their conversation did surprise them.

"Frances, do you always wear pajamas?" she asked

"Yes, Miss Russell," she replied.

"And Darlene, do you always wear a nightgown?"

"Yes, Miss Russell."

"Well, really, girls, I think you should both wear nightgowns or both wear pajamas. This is much too suggestive."

Not surprisingly, Lila stayed at Drew Seminary for only one year. By the fall of 1937, after another summer session at Northwestern University and completion of her Master's degree, she became the Dean of Women at Iowa Wesleyan College in Mount Pleasant, Iowa, where she also taught courses in Education and in Psychology while Mildred attended Mount Pleasant High School. They shared a two-room apartment in the women's dormitory, Hershey Hall.

A typical schedule for Lila during her three years at Iowa Wesleyan was as follows:

6:30–7:00	Arise and dress
7:00–8:00	Breakfast; plan day; routine procedure of seeing the sick, helping students, straightening public rooms
8:00–12:00	Classes, study, chapel, interviews, office work, clubs, etc. (One hour out for rest and relaxation if possible.)

12:00–1:00	Lunch
1:00–6:00	Flexible program: visit schools, committee work, office work, clubs, interviews, etc. (One hour out for rest and relaxation if possible.)
6:00–7:00	Dinner and recreation
7:00–10:00	Study, reading, interviews, help students or faculty. On call.
10–10:45	Close of day duties; check hall, etc.
10:45–12	Prepare lessons for next day's classes

Her notes, with the above schedule say: "A dean of women who is in charge of a residence hall and who teaches from 8 to 12 hours a week must have a rather flexible program. I have regular routine daily duties, but I am subject to call at any time in case of an emergency. My efficiency is greatest between 8 A.M. and Noon, and again after 10:30 P.M. when the house is quiet. I have no regular play habits. I usually go to a show once a week; I am asked to chaperone parties about once a week; I go for a drive almost every day; I average a speech a week to civic or religious organizations, and a tea or dinner once a week or more, some for pleasure, some for duty."

Lila had been successful in attaining her original goals and one of her professors suggested that, since she would now be teaching in a college, it might be expedient for her to work toward a Ph.D. She was incredulous, but decided she would try to do that. She had been elected to Pi Lambda Theta, the Education honorary, and had branched out in her social activities, including learning to dance and attending social functions of faculty groups. She now had a two-fold objective: to get her Ph.D. and to earn a living to support herself and her daughter doing satisfying work. She wanted to continue in the counseling and guidance of young people and her post as Dean of Women at Iowa Wesleyan allowed that interest to be followed.

Lila & Raymond, 1962

SECOND MARRIAGE

It was customary, when Lila lived in India, for her to entertain guests from America who came to Darjeeling. Weather permitting, she would take them to Tiger Hill, the nearest site from which the tip of Mount Everest could be seen. She also generally exchanged Christmas cards with such visitors in the years that followed.

One such visitor was a professor of Philosophy and Religion from Syracuse University, Raymond Piper. Dr. Piper was traveling to various locations in the orient visiting the sites associated with the oriental religions. One of the missionaries in Calcutta brought him up to Darjeeling and asked Lila to take him to see the sunrise on Mt. Everest. This was not an unusual request. Lila had the use of the school car, and she would drive with her guests to Ghoom, a hill station where they would leave the car and start the climb.

She told the missionary to have Dr. Piper at the car at 2:30 a.m. He was there, and as they drove, Lila learned that he was a professor of Philosophy at Syracuse University and that he was primarily interested in religions of the people. The people of Darjeeling and the surrounding area were mostly Buddhists, but a very different form of Buddhism from that found in Japan, China, and the Eastern Orient, which he had already visited and studied.

At that time, the population of Mt. Hermon School included not only Americans, British, and other Europeans, but also Anglo-Indians, a few Chinese and Tibetans, many of mixed parentage, and a few Indian children.

Learning of his interest, Lila suggested that he might like to visit a lamasary. There were two Tibetan girls in the upper classes at Mt. Hermon and they had taken Lila to observe various rituals in a local lamasery. On one occasion during a Pujah, a major religious celebration, they had invited her to go with them to their lamasery when the Dalai Lama was to be in Ghoom to baptize their baby brother. On that occasion, Lila had met the Dalai Lama. The occasion was especially memorable to her because she was privileged to be the only white woman to have this rare opportunity.

The climb up to the place from which the peak of Mt. Everest can be seen is a long, arduous climb, but they reached their destination before the sun was up. They opened their lunch bags, ate, and exercised to keep warm, all the time watching the sky gradually brightening and finally the clouds clearing. It was a gloriously beautiful sunrise. First the sunbeams touched Kinchenjunga, then other peaks, and finally there was Mt. Everest. The mountain has been reported to be 29,002 feet high and, from Tiger Hill, people say they can see the top two feet.

Lila had made the trip to Tiger Hill to see the sunrise on Mt. Everest on many occasions. Others had sometimes gone up and the cloud cover hid the mountain, but when Lila went up, it never failed to make its glorious appearance. She always found it an awesome sight, which made her feel uplifted and yet very humble. Dr. Piper was exalted by the sight! Lila said it was one of the really perfect sunrises on Mt. Everest that she had seen, and she had taken groups to Tiger Hill in every one of the nine years she was in India.

An interesting side note: During Lila's last year in India, one of the students in the group going to Tiger Hill suffered an epileptic seizure when the group was still at the Ghoom station. Lila sent the group on ahead to Tiger Hill while she stayed at the station with the student. On that occasion, the group did not see Mt. Everest.

After seeing the sunrise, Lila took Dr. Piper to the Bazaar in Darjeeling where she helped him buy some very unusual and lovely curios. Little did she know that a few years later, they would be added to her own collection of Indian and Tibetan curios.

While she was teaching at Drew Seminary in 1935-36, one of her senior students said that she was going to study at Syracuse after graduating from Drew. Lila told her that if she ever took a course with Dr. Piper, she should tell him she had been a student of Lila's. Not only did she take a course with Dr. Piper, she took every course he taught and she was instrumental in bringing them back together.

On June 7, 1940, Lila married Dr. Raymond Frank Piper, professor of Philosophy at Syracuse University in the Iowa Wesleyan chapel with Mildred as her maid-of-honor. Mildred had just graduated from Mount Pleasant High School. That marked the end of Lila's career as a Dean of Women and the end of her doctoral studies. She had completed her course work, passed the required language exams, and had a dissertation topic, so she became what is known as an ABD—All But Dissertation. She moved to Syracuse, New York, and the next chapter of her life began.

Dr. Piper had been married before and divorced from his first wife. They had two adopted children, a girl named Laurine and a boy named Edward, who had both left home by the time Lila and Raymond were married. Mildred was away attending Carleton College in Minnesota, so Lila and Raymond rented a one-bedroom apartment at 606 University Avenue within walking distance of the University. The apartment also had an alcove where they put a studio couch, dresser, and desk for Mildred's use when she was home from college.

At first Lila was busy getting acquainted and involved in her new community. She and Raymond were both active in University United Methodist Church, the church in which Norman Vincent Peale had formerly been the pastor. Raymond often taught the adult section of Sunday School. Lila also taught Sunday School, and eventually became the Sunday School Superintendent and a member of the Church's Board.

On one early occasion at the church, the woman who was president of the Women's Christian Temperance Union (WCTU) approached Lila about becoming a member. While Lila did not smoke or drink, her response to the president was, "I believe in Temperance in ALL things, but that does not mean abstinence." Needless to say, she did not join.

Lila loved the stained glass windows of the church, which depicted stories from the Bible. She enjoyed taking visitors on tours of the church and explaining the windows to them. Later in her life, she recorded her narrative describing the windows and it was published and re-published by the church.

As a professor, Raymond was very conscientious about his research and teaching. He and a colleague at Syracuse had published a book, *The Fields and Methods of Knowledge*, and when he married Lila he had started gathering materials for another book to be called *Cosmic Art*. He always carried a pencil stub and some 3x5 cards in his jacket pocket. They were used cards that he got either from the University Library or from the Registrar's Office. When an idea struck him that might be of later use in a class or in his book, he would pull out the pencil and a card and make note of it in Gregg shorthand. He was very skilled in shorthand.

Raymond had a nervous habit of clearing his throat frequently when he spoke before groups. This was true in his classes at the University and also in other settings, such as the Sunday School classes that he taught. But he was a popular professor, generally patient with his students and always interested in their progress.

Another of Raymond's characteristics was his deep interest in ESP and spiritualism. He would visit a spiritualist medium from time to time, and sometimes give full credence to their comments and suggestions. In one instance, when there were two candidates for an open position in the Philosophy Department, he visited a medium and then pursued the candidate that she had recommended. He read all of Edgar Cayce's books and his thinking was influenced by them.

Lila and Mildred had not had to share each other from the time Royce died in 1925 until Mildred came home from her first year of college in 1941. By then, Lila and Raymond had worked out a pattern of living into which Mildred had to fit. There were stresses and strains and life was not always peaceful, but Mildred's part in the friction was not continuous. She returned to Carleton College in Minnesota for her sophomore year in 1941-42. By the fall of 1942, World War II was in full swing, travel was difficult, and she could receive free tuition at Syracuse University as Raymond's step-daughter, so she transferred. At Syracuse, she lived in one of the women's dormitories the first semester of her junior year, until the need for housing for other students forced her to move back to Lila and Raymond's apartment. In her senior year, she lived in the Alpha Chi Omega sorority house, a sorority she had joined during her junior year.

Lila, 1943—Director of Civil Defense Volunteer Office

JOBS IN SYRACUSE

In March, 1941, Lila was appointed Secretary of Civilian Mobilization. At that time, the Volunteer Service Bureau of the Syracuse Council of Social Agencies began its program of expansion to build up the civilian protection organization. Later, the program became the Civil Defense Volunteer Office (CDVO) of the Syracuse War Council. In that job, Lila was responsible for over-seeing the recruitment, training, and assignment of civilian volunteers.

No clippings are available to describe Lila's work during the first nine months of her work in that job, but at a special luncheon meeting, on December 5, 1941, over 200 men and women gathered to hear a report on progress of the office in its first year. At the luncheon, a telegram was read from Mrs. Eleanor Roosevelt, wife of the President, in which she congratulated the Syracuse office on being one of the first in the country and on having a long record of achievements. In Lila's report at that luncheon, she said that from a registration of 130 volunteers the year before, the enrollment had jumped to 6,000. She reported that 2,000 of these had taken a first aid course with 44 new instructors for additional teaching already trained. In addition, 250 people had completed home nursing, with 30 teachers trained; 141 had completed the "Gray Ladies" course, 25 the nutrition course, and 60 were currently enrolled in the Nurses' Aid course.

Other courses being conducted under the auspices of the volunteer office included a recreation leaders' course, a motor corps and motor mechanics' course, a staff assistants' course, knitting, office work, and surgical dressings work. There were 1500 wardens registered, 800 more were in training, and 3,000 were needed. There were 700 volunteer policemen, 325 in training, and 1,000 more needed.

For her job as Director of the CDVO, Lila had a military-type uniform, which she often wore when she made her frequent speeches throughout the county. Her topic on many occasions was "Women's Place in the War Effort." In one of her speeches, she said:

There is something for everyone to do to win this war. We must feel that the job we are doing is important and significant in the war effort. Sometimes it takes imagination to see where we fit into the total effort, but every man, woman and child can have a part. We must be articulate about what we are fighting for. It is the war of the people and we must make the peace.

She cited some of the things that women could do to help win the war: work in war industries, volunteer jobs, home child care, nutrition, salvage, and recreation work. She also pointed out that women were responsible for morale and could help to prevent inflation by investing in bonds instead of spending.

In recruiting interceptor command volunteers, Lila announced these qualifications: Applicants must be citizens, men or women, between the ages of 18 and 45. They must have good hearing, good vision, good telephone voice, good health, be more than 5'3" tall, slim type preferred. They must be able to work a four or five hour shift. Most needed were:

- Housewives who can work shifts from 7 a.m. to 12:30 p.m. or from 8 a.m. to 1:30 p.m.

- Students and women without jobs who can work from 12:30 to 6 or 1:30 to 7 p.m.

- Professional business women or teachers who can work from 6 to 11 or 7 to 12 p.m.

- Men, two nights a week, from 11 p.m. to 7 a.m. and 12 midnight to 8 a.m.

Lila also reminded her audiences that a woman's first defense job was in her home. She told them that studies of juvenile delinquency showed that the broken home is its major cause. It didn't matter if the home was broken because of divorce or because the mother was spending all her time outside. She reminded women that there were plenty of things that could be done at home to aid the defense effort: salvage, budgeting, belt-tightening, and the saving of spendings to put into bonds and war stamps. Meanwhile, there were thousands of jobs in defense to be filled by volunteers. The jobs were less glamorous than jobs before the war actually broke out but they were more real, she said, and they were going to be more and more real as time went on. She said, "I think we'll all forget how to play bridge before this war is over."

By March, 1942, 13,000 volunteers had registered for service in Syracuse and Onondaga County. Women were particularly volunteering for work in child care, case work, clinics, communications, nursing personnel work, dramatics, and dietetics.

In one of her speeches, Lila asked her audience these questions: Did you buy a lot of hose when you heard there was to be a silk shortage? Are your shelves stacked with coffee? Do you have more sugar than you can use? In other words, are you helping to win this war, or helping to lose it?

In the summer of 1942, volunteers recruited by the Volunteer Office canvassed every one of the 3200 merchandising establishments in Syracuse and the 1200 similar businesses in the county. Each enterprise was supplied with printed instructions from the U.S. government's Office of Price Administration regarding the manner in which they were to post their "ceiling prices."

Also in the summer of 1942, 80 volunteer clerical workers assisted in the "supplemental sugar rationing registration" which rationed extra sugar for canning purposes. Another 20 volunteer typists assisted the Oswego coast guard unit in the registration of boat users.

The Syracuse office was copied by many cities all over the country, with representatives coming to Syracuse to study its plans and operations. In the fall of 1942, Lila completed a "Volunteer Office Handbook," a manual for interviewers and other workers of the volunteer office staff.

On January 31, 1943, the Syracuse newspapers announced Lila's resignation from her War Council Post.

Lila's next job was working as a counselor with the Child Care Committee of Syracuse's War Council. That group was charged with responsibility for setting up a coordinated community program for the care of children in war time. Cooperating were all of the local peace-time child care agencies.

The free counseling service was provided for working mothers to help them make good plans for their children while the mothers were at work. The care might be a foster day home for the baby, a day nursery or nursery school for preschool children, a recreation program and out-of-school supervision for the school-age boy and girl, a neighbor who gives "homemaker service," or a combination of several of these services for the mother with several children. In each case, the mother retained full responsibility for her children, paid for their care, and kept them at home except during her working hours. A newspaper article commented, "Thanks to this program, Syracuse will not have any 'Orphans of Production'." This free counseling service was provided weekday mornings at the local United States Employment Service office, and afternoons at the YWCA.

By June 1, 1943, six child care centers had enrolled 140 children of war-working parents, with more centers being planned. Funds for the operation of the schools were provided by a Lanham Act grant, and parents paid 50 cents per day for a "short day" and 75 cents for a longer one. The schools were in operation 12 hours a day, 6:30 A.M. to 6:30 P.M., or 7 A.M. to 7 PM.

A newspaper article in December, 1943, described in some detail the arrangements for care of smaller children in day nurseries, day care centers, and foster homes. The Child Care Centers were under the supervision of trained, paid workers. Regular medical check-ups were part of the program. Hot meals were planned by expert nutritionists; recreation and guidance was under the supervision of women trained in, and specializing in, child care. The children followed certain programs. Part of each day's plan included cod liver oil and naps. Playground equipment and playmates helped to keep the children contented. Foster day homes were provided for children under the age of two. Nursery schools took care of children aged two to five. Children could be left at child care centers from 7 in the morning until 7 at night, with the assurance of good care, good meals, and good times. Some children were at play centers for holiday periods only. Fees were nominal and covered only the actual cost of the food. Cod liver oil, blankets, and other necessities were provided by clubs and civic organizations.

As a result of Lila's experience with the day care program in Syracuse, she was hired by the State of New York to take charge of day care centers for the children of women in the work force throughout the State, from Montauk Point to Buffalo. Travel was extremely difficult in those days. Trains and buses were crowded and often without schedules because of military needs. Gas was rationed, so she couldn't drive her own car the length and breadth of the State. Her solution to this was interesting. She rented a room in Albany, where she had her office, returning home only on weekends. Mildred, who had transferred to Syracuse University by that time, kept house for Raymond. With all the time Lila had to wait for trains and buses, she resumed one of her youthful pursuits, crocheting. She crocheted over 100 very attractive and very popular cordé purses during the war for friends, for family, and for sale.

During one of her winters in Albany, Lila slipped on the ice and broke her ankle. When it had been set, she resumed her work and travel. Since she used public transportation anyway, her inability to drive with a cast failed to limit her productivity. By the time the war was over, she was Director of the Child Care Division of the New York State Youth Commission.

After the war, Lila returned to Syracuse where she continued working. In the spring of 1948, she was appointed Director of the Onondaga Council of Campfire Girls, Inc. which served Syracuse and Onondaga County. Lila was very skillful at many crafts and she applied those skills in her work with the Campfire groups.

When Lila started working with Campfire Girls, their total membership in the county was 500 girls and 20 active leaders. By March of 1952, when she resigned, there were 1800 girls and 150 active leaders. One of the major improvements made under her leadership was in the camping facilities, which were enlarged to accommodate more than twice as many campers as before, with nine new cabins, new docks, and better sports and game facilities. Another major improvement was a much sounder financial position.

During her tenure, greater emphasis was placed on community service by Camp Fire Girls. The girls gave help to community agencies while earning their citizenship honors. For instance, they helped with the March of Dimes, Christmas Seals, Community Chest, Liberty Bell, and other county-wide fund drives. The most extensive community service project was the annual Christmas Council Fire, for which Camp Fire Girls made and gave several hundred gifts to needy and hospitalized children as well as to other groups. Other community service activities included the giving of gifts to residents of the County Home on Valentine's Day, St. Patrick's Day, Thanksgiving, and Christmas.

Lila told a newspaper interviewer that her most enjoyable moments during her four years with Camp Fire Girls were those spent sitting on the floor in a circle with the girls to sing or to teach symbols, on hikes or camping trips, or while playing games.

In early 1951, Lila and Raymond bought a home at 1310 Comstock Avenue, in Syracuse. It was the first time Lila had owned a home and she loved it. It had a basement, where she did the wash and stored her canned goods and frozen foods. It even had a fruit cellar under the garage which she filled with her products. She also produced dozens of crafts in her basement.

The ground floor of the house had a living room, dining area, kitchen, two bedrooms, one bathroom, and an attached garage. The upper floor had a study and an attic. Raymond had his study on the upper floor where he worked on his *Cosmic Art*.

When Lila and Raymond moved to their new home, Mildred (then known as Mickey) and her husband, Jim Leonard, moved into the apartment at 606 University Avenue. They had been married in 1947, and their marriage broke up in 1951. Mickey stayed in the apartment and another graduate student, Adaleen Burnett, moved in with her to share expenses.

◆   ◆   ◆

In August, 1952, Lila became Executive Director of Syracuse Girls Club. When Lila joined the staff, the club was meeting at the Vocational High School. Under her leadership, many changes took place and the program was expanded.

By the time she resigned in August 1957, the club was meeting five days a week in its own building, to which a recreation room had been added through the generosity of one of the city's women's service groups. The Club's membership was over 300, a Mothers Club had been formed, and Day Camps had been developed to meet a need during the summer months.

◆   ◆   ◆

Lila, 1947

In 1953, Mildred (by then known as Kitty) was married to Raymond A. Katzell, an industrial psychologist. They lived in an apartment in Jackson Heights, Queens, New York. Kitty, who had earned an M.A. in Counseling Psychology at Syracuse, had a job at Macy's as Supervisor of Employee Testing. From 1954 to 1973, she worked for the National League for Nursing in their Division of Measurement and Evaluation. While working there, she completed a Ph.D. in Psychological Measurement and Evaluation at Columbia University in 1967. In 1973 she became vice-president of the Professional Examination Service, another testing company in New York. Later that year, and until her retirement in 1981, she was on the staff of the Professional Examinations Division of The Psychological Corporation.

It might be noted that Lila adapted to Mildred's various name changes. When Mildred became "Mickey" in high school, and later when Ray nick-named her "Kitty", Lila accepted each of the new names and used them in correspondence and in personal conversations.

At the time of their marriage, Kitty's husband, Ray, was Vice-President of Richardson, Bellows, Henry & Co., an industrial psychological consulting organization. From 1957 until his retirement as a professor emeritus in 1984, he was a Professor of Psychology at New York University, during nine years of which he served as Head of the Psychology Department. In 1956, he and Kitty bought a home in Glen Cove, New York, where they lived until 1989 when they moved to a continuing care retirement community, Medford Leas, in Medford, New Jersey. From 1965 to 1981, they also had an apartment in Greenwich Village from which Ray could walk to his office at the University, and Kitty could get the subway at the corner of their block to reach her office. Ray died in 2003.

◆   ◆   ◆

Throughout Lila and Raymond's married life, Raymond continued working on his book, *Cosmic Art*. His objective at first was to determine if there were living artists who were objectifying their philosophical, religious, and later, psychic insights in aesthetic forms. He corresponded with over 2000 artists from 64 countries and gathered over 2500 prints of their works, supported by artists' statements, personal histories, and inspirational writings.

To gather the information he needed for *Cosmic Art*, Raymond used an unconventional questionnaire to supplement the biographical material and educational background for each artist. He asked them to answer six questions:

1. Can you formulate the special symbolic meanings in your work?

2. Please put down a frank, clear, compact statement of the mood, sentiment, idea, or vision which you experienced.

3. Please name any religious, metaphysical or occult society, organization, or movement in which you are, or have been, actively interested, and indicate its effect upon your viewpoint and art.

4. If you have had any extraordinary mystical, or aesthetic or psychic experience, or conceptions of God, beauty, or the spiritual life, which might explain your creations, would you kindly summarize them.

5. Please state briefly your idea of God, of man, and of man's goal or purpose in existence.

6. If you have formulated any striking or illuminating aphorisms or maxims about art, religion, or God, please record them.

Ingo Swan, who assisted with the publication of *Cosmic Art,* reported that all of the 850 artists "whose works form the nexus of (Raymond's) inquiry" reported at length on their special experiences which, as the years proceeded, gave rise to their particular visions.

Lila and Raymond's home was decorated with some of the cosmic paintings and he talked about this interest of his at every opportunity. In preparation for *Cosmic Art* and to generate interest in the subject, he first wrote and published a smaller volume, *The Hungry Eye.* While it was never a best-seller, in a sense it paved the way for *Cosmic Art.* At this writing, in 2006, both books are listed with Amazon.com.

Raymond died on December 31, 1962. He and Lila had spent a pleasant Christmas holiday with Mildred and her husband in Glen Cove, New York. On December 31, Lila was in the kitchen and Raymond was lying on the couch in the living room when she thought she heard him say something to her. He often spoke from the living room when she was in the kitchen and she often asked him not to do that because she couldn't always hear what he was saying. When she went into the living room to ask what he had said, she discovered that he had died. He apparently had suffered a massive stroke. The mailman arrived at that precise moment and stayed with Lila despite her protestations that he should be about his duties.

Lila and Raymond had both arranged that their bodies should be given to the Syracuse University medical school, so there were no funeral arrangements to be made. Kitty came and stayed with Lila for a few days to help her with some of the many details to be handled at such a time.

◆　　　◆　　　◆

In 1968, Lila started losing weight. She was having trouble with her digestion. Her physician put her on Maalox, but it didn't seem to solve the problem. One Sunday in church one of her friends, a physician, commented on her weight loss. She told him what had been going on and he asked her to come and see him.

He discovered that she had intestinal cancer. She had successful surgery, and returned to her usual busy life in her own home, but never regained the weight she had lost. Kitty came from New York and stayed with her for a time during her hospitalization and her convalescence.

◆　　　◆　　　◆

Lila had become very well known in Syracuse and Onondaga County and was named one of eleven "Women of Achievement" by the Syracuse *Post-Standard* newspaper in 1963, when she was recognized for her contribution to international friendship. Beginning in 1966, she was listed in *Who's Who of American Women*. She was a member of Pi Lambda Theta, women's education honorary society. Among her many local activities, Lila was a member of the Syracuse Business and Professional Women's Club, Zonta, the National League of American Pen Women, Friends of Reading, International Platform Association, and AARP, serving as president of each at some time. She was the only woman member of the Monarch Club, a local men's service club, and she served as president of the Women's Society for Christian Service of the University United Methodist Church.

◆　　　◆　　　◆

After Raymond's death at the end of 1962, Lila determined to pursue the completion of *Cosmic Art*. He had devoted many hours over many years to the book and she felt that it needed to be finished. With the cooperation and assistance of a friend, Ingo Swan, the book was finally published by Hawthorn Books in 1975. It contains 152 pages, with 18 color plates and 94 black and white illustrations. In its initial printing, it sold for $16.50.

Lila, 1973

Lila conducting Graphoanalysis class

GRAPHOANALYSIS

Lila's long-lasting love affair with Graphoanalysis began in 1957 when she was arranging a program for Zonta, a professional Woman's service club to which she belonged. When searching for "something different" for the program, she scheduled the only graphoanalyst in Syracuse for the lecture. Lila was immediately interested and told Raymond that she intended to investigate, and, if she found anything promising in it, she would take the course. She felt that if Graphoanalysis proved to be authentic, it would be a useful tool in her work as a counselor.

Raymond, by then retired from Syracuse University, was writing a book on Cosmic Art for which he had corresponded with people all over the world. When these people visited the Pipers, Lila found that some of them were not what their letters had suggested. With this laboratory right in her home, Lila enrolled in the general course. To test the accuracy of Graphoanalysis, she wrote brief one- or two-page analyses of 100 of her husband's correspondents scattered over the United States, Australia, New Zealand, Asia, Africa, and Europe. In her analyses, she told the writers what she had found in their writing and asked them to write and tell her where she was right and where she was wrong, explaining that she was studying Graphoanalysis. Incredibly, she heard from almost every one of them. Most comments were like, "It's uncanny," "You told me things I didn't know about myself." And "I know myself much better now."

Since Lila had been involved in organization work in Syracuse since 1940, she was already well known. She had sold the community on volunteer services to Child Care, Camp Fire Girls, and Girls Club. Now she sold them on Graphoanalysis. At first, she did this mostly through talks, averaging about 75 a year. Through those contacts came requests for individual personal analyses, compatibility reports, and other types of analyses.

After she had spoken to a men's service club, one of the members asked her to help him with his employee hiring as the turnover was too great. She had never done that but told him she'd like to try. They worked out a system, and she was his consultant for more than a year until he was transferred from Syracuse.

While she was doing that work, the manager would drop off applications at her home and pick them up when her analyses were finished. Usually Lila gave them to him without comment, but one evening she had a report on the top of the pile that showed excellent traits. When she gave the manager the folders, she said, "This man's writing shows that he likes variety and change, probably the type who changes jobs often."

About a month later when he saw her, he asked, "Did I tell you about the one you said wouldn't stick?" "No," she said, wondering if she had made a mistake. "Did you hire him?" "Yes," he acknowledged. "And he lasted exactly ten days."

One of Lila's first questioned-document cases was for a girl in one of her Basic Steps classes who had been getting anonymous letters and cards over a long period, all mailed from different places. She brought these to Lila, along with other letters from several of her boy friends. The girl had been positive that the person Lila had identified could not be the culprit, so it took quite a while to close the case. Finally, one evening she brought two more cards, one signed by the boyfriend Lila suspected and the other an unsigned message. The final proof lay in the fact that on the unsigned card was the imprint of the signature on the signed card, as clear as an engraving. It was the man Lila had named long before.

In 1967, Lila was named Graphoanalyst of the Year by the International Graphoanalysis Society. Until 1976, at age 80, she was still actively involved with Graphoanalysis, helpng with personnel selection for an out-of-state firm, writing various kinds of analyses, teaching Basic Steps classes to others interested in learning about Graphoanalysis, giving illustrated talks about this work, and analyzing questioned documents for court cases.

Her experience in court was interesting. She was contacted by a lawyer in another New York community.

Was she familiar with questioned documents? She had dealt with anonymous letters, checks, and check endorsements.

What did she charge for her opinions? $25.

Could she examine a document in question right away? He needed a written opinion on Monday; this was Friday, exactly one week before Christmas. Lila pointed out that both he and the specimens to be examined were 100 miles away from Syracuse. The specimens would have to be carefully photographed and enlarged before they could be analyzed. The following day was Saturday and most service shops would be closed. Besides, she was busy with pre-holiday activities.

The lawyer was not to be put off. He would have the enlargements made that day and get all the documents to her first thing Saturday morning.

True to his word, the lawyer's secretary arrived at Lila's door at 10 A.M. Saturday with blow-ups of the signatures she was to compare. During their conversation, the secretary told Lila who the "other side" had brought in as their expert on questioned documents. It was the man who had written the book, *Questioned Documents*, and had testified in the Lindbergh kidnap trial. Lila did not ask for more information. She went to work and worked steadily until 1:00 A.M. Sunday producing an 8-page document.

The case concerned a last will and testament. Genuine signatures, affixed to an old will and to a number of securities over a period of years, were compared to the signature on the contested document, signed a matter of days before the person's death.

The lawyer's secretary had stayed in Syracuse overnight, so by 9:30 A.M. Sunday, the secretary was on her way back with Lila's opinion and a summary of her training and experience.

Lila was then summoned to appear in court on Tuesday morning. The hearing was held in the oldest court house in the United States. She was finally sworn in after 2:00 P.M. The lawyer questioned her in detail about her education and experience before bringing out the exhibits—the signatures she had studied. She was asked to tell the court how she had come by her decision that the signature on the contested will was genuine.

One of the defense lawyers objected, and asked for permission to question the witness as he did not consider her an expert. Permission was granted, and his first question was "Mrs. Piper, how old are you?" In Lila's view, that was his big mistake! It made her angry, but she answered. By then, she was 69. He continued to question her education, her experience, her qualifications. At some point in her responses, she mentioned her early work in the bank where her duties included examining check signatures and endorsements.

Finally, he asked her to tell about an analysis she had done recently, so she related an incident that had occurred during a recent speaking engagement when members of the audience submitted handwriting specimens for what she called "spot analyses". She told the audience that one of the specimens was written by a person whose name was different from the one on the sample she was to analyze. After she gave her views on what the writing indicated, an elderly man had stood up, admitted that the handwriting was his and that he had indeed signed a name not his own. He announced what his real name was and said that Lila had been correct on all counts in her spot analysis. He then asked if she knew who he was. Lila said she did not. He then disclosed that he was a retired justice of New York State's Supreme Court.

The trial judge finally overruled the objection and stated that he considered Lila qualified to testify.

Lila was on the witness stand almost two hours but when it was all over, she felt she had really enjoyed the experience. She even had a kind word from the opposition attorney who had done the objecting and cross-examining. After court adjourned, he assured her that there was nothing personal in his questioning of her abilities, and he added, "Now you are an expert. You have given testimony in court."

Lila never learned how the case was settled.

THE FINAL CHAPTER

In the 1970's, Lila completed Raymond's *Cosmic Art* book and continued to teach classes in Graphoanalysis, but her friends and neighbors began to notice changes in her behavior. She sometimes failed to keep appointments; she telephoned people at ungodly hours in the middle of the night; she drove at 25 mph in the left lane on the super-highway. After a time, one of her neighbors wrote and told Mildred something was wrong. Mildred was still working full time and had not been seeing Lila often enough to realize how much she had changed.

When Mildred visited, she found that Lila was not eating properly, so she ordered Meals-on-Wheels to be delivered. A week later, when she phoned Lila to find out how it was going, Lila reported that she had cancelled the delivery. Mildred scolded her and told her she needed to eat those meals, but Lila explained that they regularly served peas and she didn't like peas.

Next, Mildred found that Lila had designated someone in her church to have Power-of-Attorney for her. She had also sold some of the treasures she had brought back from India. Members of her first husband's family came to visit one time, having phoned the day before to say they would be there. When they arrived, Lila was surprised to see them. Also, Lila's appearance had changed so much that they would not have recognized her but for her smile.

Lila was aware that her memory was failing. Every day, she forced herself to do the crossword puzzle in the daily paper. She would sit on the couch in her living room with the dictionary beside her and work for as long as it took to do each puzzle. On occasion, when she was with Mildred, she would say "Oh, how I miss my mind."

In 1977, Lila moved from her beloved house to an apartment at 753 James Street in Syracuse. Friends helped her move and settle, and her designated power-of-attorney handled the sale of her house. When Mildred visited her in the apartment, she found four cans of copper polish under Lila's kitchen sink. Lila had a large Tibetan copper tea kettle which she kept polished so she must have thought she needed copper polish. Lila had a sofa bed for Mildred to sleep on when she visited. Mildred would wake in the night to find Lila standing over her not knowing who was sleeping on her sofa bed. Lila would order items from catalogs and, when they came, she would leave the packages outside her door to be returned, not knowing that she had ordered them. A dear friend at the church kept tabs on Lila, visiting almost daily. One time she wrote a note with lipstick on Lila's mirror, saying "Call Nancy." When Nancy returned the next time she found that Lila had written in lipstick, under the earlier message, "Who's Nancy?"

By this time, it was obvious that Lila needed closer supervision and that friend, Nancy, facilitated her move to a temporary facility until Mildred could make other arrangements. There was a fine nursing home in Glen Cove, where Mildred and her husband lived, and they were able to arrange for Lila to move there during 1978. She had a private room in the nursing home with a few pieces of her own furnishings, as well as pictures and books of her choosing. Lila accepted the arrangement quite graciously, perhaps because she knew she would be able to see Mildred at least once a week, whereas in Syracuse, she saw her infrequently.

Mildred and her husband tried to arrange stimulating activities to share with Lila on the weekends when they were in Glen Cove. Mildred would take Lila to the supermarket when she did her shopping. They would take Lila out for dinner and to their home. Mildred took care of Lila's laundry, which provided another topic for conversation.

The nursing home also provided some of the typical activities for the residents, Bingo, group singing, entertainers, and the like. But Lila missed some of the things that had been part of her life when she had lived alone. She had worked in a bank after college and she had always had a bank account. There was a bank across the street from the nursing home and one day she crossed the street and went in to open an account. Another time, she wandered away from the nursing home and was brought back by the local police who had found her down town in Glen Cove. The local physician who attended to Lila eventually told Mildred that the diagnosis was Alzheimer's. It was the first she had heard the term.

At this time, Mildred and her husband were still working in New York, where they had an apartment that they occupied during the week, returning to Glen Cove on weekends. They also had a pet cat, Snowflake, who was always kept indoors or on a leash, so she would be there when it was time to go to their other abode. One Sunday afternoon, when Lila was visiting at their home, she opened the back door and let Snowflake go out in the yard. The cat wandered about until Mildred realized what had happened. When she went out to bring the cat back, Snowflake went up the nearest tree. Eventually, of course, she was brought down, but that episode showed Mildred that Lila needed constant supervision.

After Lila died, Mildred found a packet of notes Lila had written, seemingly to members of her family. The notes had been written in ink on 4x6" pieces of paper

The handwriting was tiny and quite unlike her former writing. In her Graphoanalysis talks, she had often said that very small handwriting indicated deep concentration. The second of the notes reproduced below has the date August 31, 1978 on it, and Lila comments that the next week she would become an octogenarian. Her birthday was October 9, and she turned 80 in 1976. The fourth note starts with the comment "Today I am 90 years old"; she died in 1986 at the age of 89. The sixth note starts thus: "Sunday, I think And I think it is Saturday the 8" and my birthday" but her birthday was on the 9th of October.

Most of the notes were undated, so it is impossible to know in what order she wrote them, but many indicate "Sunday", the day on which she had regularly written her "family letter" to her sisters. The pattern had been established when she first went away to college and continued for the rest of her life. The notes are reproduced here. They give clear evidence of the Alzheimer's confused mind.

Sunday a.m. 5:15 a.m.

Dear Elsie & family—

I have neglected all correspondence since Elsie dispensed with all my letters when I was ill. Guess the M.D. told her I was ill. I went there once and the M.D. did not accept me as ill. And I have just got along but I miss so many things. All the family letters and each others comments. I don't have any "correspondent quarter" to use for mail or to take care of correspondence. I had this small paper lying here & I just took it to write and I write too small! There's no place here to write so it is easier to just make excuses. I'm hoping when Elsie comes to see me I can get the harness removed! I used to write them a form or more of family & friend letters every week and I miss them. See how my writing has changed! I don't feel as if I can write larger. I wonder why. My home space is so small, perhaps. I did write a note to Alta, I think just recently. No table is not conducive to letter writing.

I haven't seen loads of my friends for a year and I'm going to try to get back in some of my activities & interests. But it is not easy. Just writing this letter is an impossible job almost.

Now I must try to get back in touch with my good friends. I miss them terribly but seem impossible to make the important move. Hope you & the rest of the family are all fine & prospering.

All Love, Lila

Alta & family—send to Alta
Sunday A.M.
August 31, 1978

In just one week and a day, I'll be a whole year older and that means an octo-genarian. But I don't <u>feel</u> any older. In fact I'm in good health. Wish I could write larger. Need a table to write on. After you cut down on all my things after I was ill, I have not bought things. But I get on fine…and my days are num-bered. I'm really having trouble writing and this will be my last letter till I can write a bit larger. This pen is not conducive to large writing & this paper is small. I had not realized how the size of my home affected the size of my other activities, etc. I'm not usually a <u>small</u> writer. I do not like tiny writing.

I don't like this writing paper & I'm going to quit. It's only six o'clock in the a.m. & this is my second letter…I haven't been receiving so many letters. Guess you all are busy. Even tho I have nothing to do, I still do keep busy. But I must become more productive in my activities.

You and all the school kids are getting back to school. I feel that <u>no one</u> needs <u>me</u> nor <u>anything</u> I can do.

All love, Lila

<u>Week end</u>
Sept. 30, 1978?

Dear Family:

I'm in my own room (35) & I'm hoping to write you a letter for the week end. I hate writing on a Book end—and then I write small & even smaller! Just fin-ished our Sunday evening dinner & I took a brief walk.

The other day, I advanced into another <u>area</u> and no one said a word. I'm trying to figure how I am financially! I am feeling fine so don't bother about <u>get well</u> cards. I'm still quite a tough customer! I even wandered into your area by error but no one beat me up & I am still at large. I am very anxious to get a statement of my finances—who has my money & where is it? I want to have <u>all</u> of my assets in my own name <u>now</u>! I am really feeling on top of all my problems & I need to keep my own money. If you still have any of mine, please let me or Alta know. We are one family we <u>trust</u> each other but <u>my</u> money is <u>mine</u> and I want to keep it that way.

I am <u>terribly</u> behind in my correspondence! I owe everyone letters! But you know I always keep you posted & I want to <u>be</u> informed, too.

I have to go through my clothes and figure what I need. I have neglected my clothes—too many problems! I must get my inventory brought up to date. I have no stationery and I <u>owe</u> letters to all of you.

I want to get all my things in order and I want to get back into <u>business</u>! I am feeling fine & I need to assume Responsibility!!! Elsie has been very helpful while I have been feeling under my <u>usual life</u>! It takes a bit of time to get back into the harness.

I need stationery, stamps and I need to take complete responsibility! You & Alta have both been most helpful & I did need support for a time. I hope I can take charge now and be the "master of my soul etc..." I have money in Elsie's hands from past jobs and I need to be on top of my responsibility . . & your case—(like me!) I want to do some sewing for Kitty & Alta—if they want it and I am <u>still</u> a devoted sister & I appreciate all you have done for me! Take care & keep in touch.

All love, Lila

 (on the back of the foregoing note, she had written the following)

I hope soon to get my permission to leave my premises & able to visit Elsie and other friends & relatives.

Love, Lila

Tues. a.m.

Dear Dad & all in family etc.

Today I am ninety (90) years Old!—not Young any more…. Its not easy getting myself back into the <u>family</u> letter habit. Its been nice to be close together so we could communicate!!

My writing gets worser & worser—every day. All these small <u>bits</u> are a part of my family letter. I'm sorry for such small writing!!! All of a sudden it just <u>hap-pened</u>. Yesterday I took a short visit to see Dad and he seems a bit better. I just saw that I had another letter started for family so you see my mental State! Stupid!! Its quite chilly here and no central heat in this area so not too comfortable. I want to get letters off to all the family while I can send an envelope to cover two or more—ha ha. I have loads of envelopes here from people I should be writing to, also. But nothing much to report and that can wait. We have all seen each other & no news to report. All love, <u>Lila</u>

<u>Dad</u>
October 3

Dear Dad, Elsie, etc…

(in margin: I'll share some letters)

don't know if I have your <u>last</u> address. I'm so in a custom of writing so small, I cant write any more. I must try to write bigger & bigger again. Nothing new to be reported as far as we are concerned. I shall be glad when we can move into our own home and begin to live again. My writing has gotten smaller & smaller. I keep trying to write my old natural scroll but this is what comes out & I don't like it at all.

Our home here has no furnace heat and the room is heated from one hot pipe—not adequate at all

I am trying to get myself back into the letter writing habit & I can't write my normal large writing—I am sorry.

I keep running into letters from different ones of this family so I am getting to know some of all of you. Wish I could get myself back to my normal size writing! This is stupid.

It's still early a.m. Each one is doing her "thing". Mostly writing letters. Wonder if I'll get back to my normal size writing. I hope so—I can't seem to write large!!!

I should be writing some family letters but writing is not easy & I have nothing to share now. Hope are all O.K. and getting back into your schedule—& I hope for me too.

Love—Lila

For Alta

Sunday, I think

And I think it is Saturday the 8" and my birthday. As soon as I sit down to write, I begin to "think small"—I don't like to write small but It just comes out that way now.

I'm enjoying and deeply appreciating this nice rest. I had not been working so hard—I just seem to be out of hand.

Who bought all the chocolates and left them here? One 2 lb box of chocolates in my bath room and another large box in the bath room. And they are not cheap candy—but delicious chocolates! (Thank you…I ate one to try it out)

When Alta comes down to see me, next time, I'm going to have her open the faucet so we'll have lots of water!

I'm anxious for the day to come when I'll be living in my own suite & have all my own things together.

Its getting dark and I have to do several other things—See how forgetful I am! How tiny I am writing

Lila

Monday a.m.

Dear Elsie. As soon as I begin to think of writing, I become confused. See how small I write—and I can't seem to feel equal to normal writing. I'm very sorry but I cant write normal writing! And this is so tiresome—I tried to write that all Big! I'm glad to be OLD so I won't have to write this small so long. I really do try to write large and you see what comes out at this end. I'm hoping to take some walks and try to get some notes telling me how I stand with all my adult relatives.

I'm wearing my white leather jacket and I feel posh in it! I'm going to try to clear my finance records too with my sisters—so I'll know exactly where I stand. See how small I write? Sorry. <u>Lila</u> I stopped there to try to figure out my "days"—I've lost a day. I think and no idea <u>where</u>! Nor how! The air is always chilly here & often <u>cold</u>! I'll welcome some warmth any time! I'm going to try out some pens but using larger (see how small I go all at once! & quite unconsciously I am going to try Elsie when I get other things done.

Sunday. A.m.

Dear Family: This is my <u>first</u> letter because I have had <u>no</u> paper. Nothing at all. We get a bed and our three meals a day and that is <u>it</u>.—except for a couple of letters I have had from you—and Elsie. She came over to see me a wee bit & that was most welcome. I have a bedroom with a single bed and our meals are provided. The people are nice but we have nothing to share & I have no one to talk with most of the time—and nothing to <u>do</u>! I have no one nor nothing. I'm just here in my bedroom & a side table and no one to converse with. No one to talk with except my Kitty. Wish you'd write WFMS & tell them…I'm just eating & trying to make a small impression. They are nice enough but they are just here—& so am I. It's not living! I make my work because I cant do <u>no</u> thing!

My sister is a missionary not to far away—and she came here once. She has a Kg class etc and has a <u>going</u> school.

My pens have all dried out over here. Will use a pencil next time. I thought <u>ink</u> would be most legible but its not a bit better. I am hoping to go over to see Charlotte if she is still over the area. The letter is not worth the postage but I want to feel a family member! Love Lila

---

Dear Family at Home etc….

No calendar so I have no idea what date it is. I have tried to keep track but no guides here.

I'm just beginning to <u>feel</u> that I am still alive. Have had absolutely nothing to do <u>nor</u> anything to do with. I don't even earn my room & Board.

I have a room with a single bed & a 3-shelf T.V (?) shelf (no T.V.) a 3-V shelf holds the electric lite & clock and the very little news or other reading—my Mt. Kenchenjunga is on the wall & Dad's picture. No school, nothing here so far. Boring to say the least. I have <u>had</u> absolutely <u>no</u> mail from W.F.M.S. nor from anyone at all. Love Lila

(on the reverse of the preceding note, she had written:
Had a card from Gammill's. She was passing thru—but we missed each other. Chilly & windy today

Love Lila

It is worth noting that she refers in some of the notes to her father, who was long since dead, and in one she says "my sister is a missionary," apparently referring to Alta who was teaching in India in the 1920's. She also refers more than once to the WFMS, the Women's Foreign Missionary Society, which had sponsored her work in India 50 years earlier. On the other hand, she speaks of Kitty, whom she had only called by that name in the more recent past.

On one occasion, one of Lila's former students came to visit her. The woman's father had been a bishop in India. Lila apparently recognized her and, although she didn't call the visitor by name, she did say something about "the bishop." But, as her memory worsened, Lila came to think that Mildred was her baby sister, Anna, who had died in 1918. On the other hand, one of the aides at the nursing home used to sing Negro spirituals to Lila when she was bathing her, and Lila would sing along, remembering all the words. Memory is a strange and wonderful thing.

Physicians will tell you that no one dies "of" Alzheimer's; they die "with" Alzheimer's. At Mildred's request, Lila's physician had recorded "DNR" on her records at the nursing home so she would not be resuscitated if she were to suffer cardiac arrest. In March 1986, Mildred and her husband went on a Caribbean cruise and, when they returned, found that Lila had developed pneumonia. She died peacefully on March 26, 1986, six and a half months short of her 90th birthday. Her body was donated, in accordance with her instructions, for medical education. When she was moved from Syracuse to the New York area, arrangements were made for her body to go to the Medical School of New York University.

On April 6, 1986, a memorial service was conducted at the University United Methodist Church in Syracuse, again in accordance with her instructions. The

Pastor and Assistant Pastor spoke and in the course of the service, those assembled sang "All Hail the Power of Jesus' Name" and "Abide With Me". The scriptures were Psalm 23 (The Lord is my shepherd), Psalm 121 (I will lift my eyes unto the hills); Ecclesiastes 3 (To everything there is a season); and selections from John 1 and 14, Romans 8, and Revelations 21. A soloist sang "How Great Thou Art" and "Crossing the Bar." The congregation recited the Lord's Prayer.

Lila, 1983

978-0-595-38973-5
0-595-38973-2

Printed in the United States
64409LVS00007B/163

9 780595 389735